PREACHING

LUKE-ACTS

Preaching Classic Texts

Preaching Apocalyptic Texts
Larry Paul Jones and Jerry L. Sumney

Preaching Job
John C. Holbert

Preaching Luke–Acts
Ronald J. Allen

PREACHING

LUKE-ACTS

RONALD J.
ALLEN

Chalice Press.
St. Louis, Missouri

Cover art: Detail from ClickArt, Christian Graphics
Cover design: Michael Foley
Art direction: Michael A. Domínguez
Interior design: Wynn Younker

This book is printed on acid-free, recycled paper.

Visit Chalice Press on the World Wide Web at
www.chalicepress.com

10 9 8 7 6 5 4 3 2 1   00 01 02 03

Library of Congress Cataloging–in–Publication Data

Allen, Ronald J. (Ronald James), 1949-
    Preaching Luke-Acts / by Ronald J. Allen.
        p.   cm. – (Preaching classic texts)
    Includes bibliographical references and index.
    ISBN 0-8272-2965-8
    1. Bible. N.T. Luke–Homiletical use.   2. Bible. N.T. Acts–Homiletical
use. I. Title.
II. Series.
BS2589.A45 2000
251–dc21   00-009000

Printed in the United States of America

*To John and Marianne McKiernan,
whose sensitivities to one another and the wider
world are a sign of the restored community
to which Luke points*

Contents

PREFACE

The gospel of Luke and the book of Acts tell the story of God's intention to restore the world community so that all relationships and situations embody the divine purposes of love and justice initially revealed in Genesis 1. Working with the gospel of Luke and the book of Acts moves me to gratitude for such communities that shape my life. In a Lukan mode, I particularly thank our household, the primary community of which I am a part, for their openness to the Spirit-filled moments when we live together as a sign of the restored world: Linda, Canaan, Genesis, Moriah, Barek, Sabbath. I am further grateful to the living God for the presence and sustenance of the Spirit in seasons when our household life is in need of restoration. I thank others who are often communities that bring the divine purposes to life: our wider family; colleagues, students, and staff at Christian Theological Seminary; the congregations that have formed my existential understanding of Christian community, especially First Christian Church (Disciples of Christ) in Poplar Bluff, Missouri, First Christian Church (Disciples of Christ) in Grand Island, Nebraska, and University Park Christian Church (Disciples of Christ) in Indianapolis, Indiana. Working with Jon L. Berquist, Academic Editor of Chalice Press, is a continuous experience of renewed world.

Introduction

The gospel of Luke and the book of Acts help the preacher address some of the deepest longings of our time, such as the search for a transcendent perspective on life, the yearning for community, the hunger for religious experience, the seeking of guidance in ethical conundrums, the anxiety that results from changes in our religious and cultural institutions, and the confusion regarding the relationship of Judaism, Christianity, and other religions.

Luke and Acts do not hand us prepackaged resolutions to such issues, but bring us into conversation with perspectives and characters that engage us as we seek to identify God's presence and purposes. Indeed, a scholar characterizes Luke and Acts as a "theology of the faithful God."[1]

Preaching Themes in the Gospel of Luke and Book of Acts

I focus on preaching *themes* in Luke and Acts.[2] The designation "theme" is not a technical category of biblical scholarship. I use *theme* to speak informally of ideas, images, associations, expressions, practices, or values that span Luke 1 through Acts 28, or significant parts thereof. A theme is introduced in Luke and then developed through Luke and Acts. (For instance, the character and work of the Holy Spirit is a theme.) We can seldom understand a theme on the basis of only one passage. Individual passages contribute to themes. Awareness of themes deepens our interpretation of individual passages.

1

How a Preacher Can Use This Book

A preacher can use this book in four ways. (1) A preacher can develop a single sermon on a theme. For example, a preacher could develop a sermon on poverty, abundance, and the Christian use of material resources. (2) A preacher can develop a series of sermons in which each sermon considers a different theme. For instance, a minister could preach successively on the realm of God, the Holy Spirit, the great reunion of the human family, the restoration of women. (3) A preacher could prepare a series of sermons on each theme, basing each sermon on a passage that enhances our understanding of the theme. For instance, I might develop a series of sermons on Lukan teaching on poverty, abundance, and the Christian relationship with material resources. (4) The thematic studies in the book may enhance a preacher's consideration of particular passages. To this end, the Appendix is a table coordinating discussion of biblical texts in this book with readings in the Revised Common Lectionary.

Methods of Interpretation

My interpretation of Luke and Acts is guided by a combination of literary and rhetorical methods, with a dollop of reader-response criticism, augmented by historical criticism and the hermeneutic of suspicion.

Literary criticism refers to a variety of approaches that share the methodology of making sense of Luke and Acts as literary works. Literary criticism analyzes the settings, plot, characters, and atmosphere. When we listen to the story, we imaginatively enter the narrative world. When we leave that world, the narrative of Jesus and the church is a lens through which we interpret our world today.

I rely particularly on *reader-response criticism*, a type of literary criticism that identifies the responses of the reader (listener) to the text. What responses are evoked through a text by means of the interworking of setting, plot, characters? How do we react to the setting? to the characters? to the turns in the plot? to the narrator's point of view?

Rhetorical criticism is similar to literary criticism in seeking to name the aims of this literature. Writers and speakers in antiquity often used particular genres for particular purposes. Genres had their own conventions. Audiences were acquainted with these genres and recognized the purpose of the speaker or writer. Awareness of rhetorical genre gives the preacher clues to the intentions of the text.

Historical criticism attempts to understand a document from the perspective of its historical context, especially how people in antiquity understood objects, places, words, phrases, ideas, characters, and literary genres. Some historical critics attempt to go behind the present text of Luke and Acts to reconstruct the historical circumstances that led to the writing of these books. These hypotheses are sometimes helpful, but they are nearly always tentative. Luke and Acts do not always provide firm data that permit us to describe in detail the situation of the churches for whom the author of Luke wrote.

The *hermeneutic of suspicion* assumes that many writers shape materials to further their own interests. Males, for instance, sometimes protect male superiority. Preachers need to expose such vested interests in these books. The community can then evaluate the degree to which these interests cohere with the gospel and the degree to which they need to be corrected in the community's use of the text today.

Important Issues in Luke and Acts

Luke and Acts address several important issues.

- Who is Jesus Christ? Luke reveals Christ as the agent through whom God is manifesting the divine realm. Acts narrates the implications for the Christian community.

- What are God's purposes through Christ and the church, and in history? These materials depict the realm of God as a universal restoration beginning with the life of the church and culminating with Jesus' return.

- What is the church? Its mission? The mission of Jesus and the apostles points to the purpose of the church. The early church embodies the restoration and testifies to it through community life and preaching.

- How are Jesus Christ and the church related to the God of Israel and to Judaism? The God of Israel is the God of

Jesus Christ and the church. The story of God's restoring purposes that begins in the Septuagint is continued through Jesus and the Christian community.

Organization of the Book

Chapter 1 considers basic issues in interpretation, while chapter 2 outlines several approaches that are important for preaching. The next chapters are studies of leading representative themes in these books. These themes include the realm (NRSV: kingdom) of God (chapter 3), the Holy Spirit (chapter 4), the great reunion of the human community (chapter 5), the restoration of women in the reign of God (chapter 6), and the faithful use of material resources (chapter 7). Each chapter identifies the theme, recalls its background in Judaism, unfolds the development of the theme in Luke and Acts, reflects on their significance for the contemporary church and world, and offers a sermon.

Other Fruitful Themes

The themes discussed in this book are only representative of a multitude of other themes from Luke and Acts that the preacher could pursue. These include the relationship of Judaism and Christianity, Luke's attitude toward civil authorities, the roles of the First Testament in Christian understanding, the journey of discipleship ("the Way"), authority in the Christian community, discerning the divine leading, repentance, life in community, suffering that results from witness, prayer, baptism, the breaking of bread, Luke's picture of Paul, laying on of hands, the return of Jesus in glory, and the relationship of Judaism and early Christianity to other philosophies and religions.[3] I hope that a preacher can use the methodology and case studies in the present book as models for tracing, understanding, and developing sermons on these other themes.

CHAPTER 1

Interpreting Luke–Acts

"Why do we have to study so much stuff we never use in preaching?" Students ask this question every fall when I teach Introduction to New Testament. Such students want to know why they have to learn so much ancient culture and history, why they have to make their way through disputes in interpretation, why they have to make use of methods of biblical criticism that all have their own esoteric vocabularies.

For a long time I replied to this question with an analogy that I heard long ago from a respected figure in biblical studies. A physician must learn chemistry in order to know how the human body functions and how it interacts with medicines. When you go to a physician for treatment, you do not need a chemistry lesson, but the physician needs to know chemistry in order to prescribe the right medicine. The relationship of the preacher, the Bible, and the congregation is much the same. The congregation may not need to know everything you know about the Bible, but you need to know the chemistry of the interpretation of the Bible in order to preach reliable biblical medicine. I counseled preachers to leave much of the methodology of biblical interpretation in the study and to use only its fruits in the pulpit.

However, several years ago I concluded that preachers could often bring some of the background chemistry of interpretation directly into the sermon for the benefit of the congregation. Many Christian communities today do not know the content of the Bible or how to interpret it. The sermon that provides background material helps the congregation overcome these deficiencies. The sermon that leaves all the methodology in the study deprives the community of the opportunity to experience the joy (and perplexity) of discovery with the preacher. By speaking with the congregation about such matters, the preacher helps to actualize the priesthood of all believers; when exposed to this material, members of the congregation often have insights that illumine the preacher and others in the community. Furthermore, encountering issues in exposition helps the congregation to realize that reading the Bible is always an act of *interpretation.* We seldom uncover the single meaning of a text. We usually have to make judgments about what we think a passage means or does not mean, keeping the door open for fresh data or perspectives that may reshape our understandings.

In this chapter, I review basic issues in the interpretation of Luke and Acts that the preacher may bring into the sermon—the narrative unity of Luke and Acts, authorship, time and place of composition, sources that the author used, the congregation and their situation, the importance of the First Testament for understanding this material, the genre of these books, and their foundational theological perspective. The preacher will not want to discuss every issue in every sermon. The preacher must rely upon exegetical, theological, and pastoral sensitivity to know when such a discussion is appropriate for a particular sermon.

The Narrative Unity of Luke and Acts

Most preachers and biblical scholars today regard Luke and Acts as one story. We need to interpret these books as a continuous narrative. In order to understand a passage or theme in Luke, we should trace its motifs into Acts. In order to understand a passage or theme in Acts, we need to consider its roots in Luke. For example, we can properly make sense of Luke's teaching about God's care for the poor in the gospel only from the perspective of the community's care for the poor in the Acts. The preacher can help the congregation avoid treating individual passages in isolation and can help the community discover Luke–Acts as an interpretive fabric in which many threads and patterns are intertwined.

Who Wrote Luke and Acts?

We can neither prove nor disprove that someone named Luke wrote these two books. Luke is not named as the author in either the gospel or the Acts. This attribution, found only in the title of the gospel ("According to Luke"), does not appear in an ancient manuscript of the gospel until 175–225 C.E. in a document called p[75]. The designation "the Acts of the Apostles" does not appear until Irenaeus (130–200 C.E.), Clement of Alexandria (150–215 C.E.), and the Muratorian Canon (late second century C.E.). Some Christians think that the title "The Acts of the Apostles" does not quite fit that book because the emphasis is not really on the apostles but on the emergence of the early Christian community as a witness to the reign of God. While a few apostles play central roles, many additional people also have prominent parts. Paul, who is not officially one of the Twelve, is the central figure after the apostolic council (Acts 15).

Some people in the Christian community think that the writer of these two volumes was a companion of Paul named Luke (mentioned in Col. 4:14; Philem. 24; 2 Tim. 4:11). Most biblical scholars think that such identification is possible, but not likely. Even if we knew that the author of these books was a companion of Paul, our ability to make sense of Luke and Acts would not be significantly enriched.

Because Colossians 4:14 depicts Luke as "the beloved physician," some Christians in previous generations thought that these books were full of medical terminology. However, societies in antiquity did not have a technical medical vocabulary. The consensus today is that Luke's language does not reflect medical background.

Many scholars think that Luke may have been a Christian Jewish person, that is, someone of Jewish origin who recognized God at work through the ministry of Jesus and the church. Others think that Luke was a Gentile. This issue cannot be settled definitively. However, Luke and Acts are so permeated by Judaism and the Septuagint, I think it likely that Luke was a Christian Jewish person.

I follow the convention of all the scholars known and speak of this writer as Luke. However, we do not know for certain who wrote Luke and Acts. This fact can directly help the preacher in a cautionary way. Individualistic twenty-first-century North American culture is fascinated by personality. Periodically I hear this fascination in the form of a first-person monologue that begins, "My name is Luke. I was with Paul and want to tell you what I experienced." Other preachers do not adopt the first-person monologue but hypothesize Luke's psychology (e.g., "Luke must have felt..."). Almost inevitably these sermons degenerate into speculations that have no basis in the text itself. The fact that we do not know anything about the author ought to prevent the preacher from engaging in such conjecture.

Time and Place of Composition

We do not know the city or even the region where Luke wrote these books. Scholars have proposed the following as possible places of composition: Achaia, Antioch, Caesarea, Ephesus, and Rome. However, neither internal evidence (from Luke and Acts) nor external (e.g., references by other writers) is convincing.

Many scholars notice that this material reveals a fine knowledge of Hellenistic urban culture. For example, in Mark 2:4, four friends carry a paralytic to Jesus for healing. Jesus is in a house, but the house is full. The friends ascend to the flat roof of a Palestinian house and dig through a thatch and mud roof to lower the paralytic to Jesus. In Luke, however, the house has a fine tile roof (Lk. 5:19). The tile roof is typical of a house in a prosperous Hellenistic urban neighborhood. Most of the events in Acts occur in urban settings.

This familiarity with Hellenistic urban culture suggests to some scholars that the author of Luke wrote outside of Palestine in an undisclosed setting in the Mediterranean world. It may also suggest a point of contact for many of today's congregations in urban settings.

The attitude toward the wider Hellenistic world in Luke–Acts is ambiguous. One the one hand, some elements in the Hellenistic setting support the Christian witness in Acts. Paul, for example, is able to travel so widely because sea voyages were possible for the middle class. Roman civil authorities sometimes protect the early Christian disciples from violence. The Roman judicial system is the mechanism by which Paul carries the gospel to Rome (e.g., Acts 19:35–43; 22:22–29). Many persons of non–Jewish origin welcome the gospel and affiliate with the church.

However, as the story of Luke–Acts unfolds, we become increasingly aware that Hellenism needs restoration. Idols, and the debased social world that accompanies them, abound. Although some Roman civil officials help the early witnesses, other civil authorities abuse and imprison Jesus and the disciples (e.g., Lk. 23:1–25; Acts 16:19–24; 18:12–17; 24:22–27). While Luke acknowledges that non-Jewish people can have some knowledge of God, Luke more forcefully emphasizes that Hellenism often leads to religious misunderstanding, idolatry, and violence (e.g., Acts 14:8–18; 18:23–40). When Jesus returns in glory, all people will be judged (Acts 17:29–31; cf. 1:10–11; 2:17–21; 10:42; 12:49–56). For the church in Acts, the Hellenistic world is a setting for mission.

We do not know when the author of Luke wrote these volumes. He did not leave traces of an exact date in either the gospel or Acts. Today's scholarly consensus is that he wrote them after Mark because Luke follows (and expands) Mark's outline. Most interpreters think that the writer took quill in hand after the Romans destroyed the temple in Jerusalem in 70 C.E., because several passages assume that this event has taken place (Lk. 13:33–35; 19:41–44; 21:20–24). Less than a hundred years later, other Christian documents cite Luke and Acts, thereby revealing that both books were in circulation. The scholarly opinion today is that Luke wrote in the decade 80–90 C.E.

The date is important for the preacher not for its own sake, but because it helps us place some of the themes in Luke–Acts against the background of events and forces of that period. I sketch some of these factors below ("The Congregation and Its Situation"). Both Luke and Acts contain vibrations set in motion by the struggles and opportunities of their historical circumstances.

Sources That Luke Used

Virtually all scholars today are convinced that the Lukan writer wrote the gospel and Acts with the help of preexisting sources. The most common explanation of this phenomenon is the two-source theory. According to this theory, Luke (and Matthew) drew on two sources as they wrote their gospels: the gospel of Mark and a source called Q (from the German word *Quelle*, "source"). Luke wove materials from these sources into the gospel of Luke. We might think of these sources as computer files that Luke combined and reworked.

However, the two-source theory does not explain materials that are found only in Luke, for example, the parable of the parent and the two children (Lk. 15:11–32). A third source (sometimes called "L") may have furnished this material; or, the Lukan author is such a fine storyteller that he could have composed them.

Almost certainly, the author of Luke also had sources when penning the Acts of the Apostles. However, they do not exist independently in the same way that Mark does. Like other writers in the Hellenistic period, the Lukan author has so rewritten the sources that we cannot ferret out pre-Lukan material on the basis of its distinctive language, grammar, or style.

Several passages in Acts are told in the first person plural, such as, "We set sail from Troas" (Acts 16:11; cf. 16:11–17; 20:5–15; 21:8–18; 27:1–28:16). Some preachers take these "we" passages to be eyewitness accounts from the experience of someone traveling with Paul–perhaps Luke. However, I take my place in a modest scholarly consensus in thinking that the "we" passages are a stylistic device that was common in the first century. Writers of the Septuagint, the translation of the Hebrew Bible into Greek, sometimes slip back and forth between first and third person in narration (e.g., Ezra 8:23–31; 8:35–9:15). Many Greek writers rehearsed journey narratives in the first person in order to intensify the effect on the listener.

The Acts of the Apostles circulated in the early church in two primary versions. (1) The Alexandrian manuscripts are remarkably similar to the version in today's Bibles. Textual critics, contemporary scholars whose specialty is the study of manuscripts of antiquity, are convinced that the Alexandrian tradition is older and more authentic. (2) The Western text amplifies the Alexandrian version by 10 percent. The Western text does not contain additional narratives, but only elaborates the stories and speeches found in the Alexandrian text. The Western text explains many details in Acts, and it elevates the titles of leading people. The Western tradition paints Jewish leaders in Acts in an even more pernicious way than the Alexandrian text.

The fact of these source traditions can help the preacher. First, they implicitly warn us against bibliolatry, that is, worshiping the Bible. Luke and Acts did not descend from heaven, but are the precipitate of complex historical processes. While the Bible is immensely helpful to us, it bears scars of relativity.

Second, the sources remind preacher and congregation that the Lukan writer's activity in putting together Luke–Acts is much like the work of today's preacher: interpreting sacred tradition in order to alert the community to the divine presence and purposes in the present. We hear Luke–Acts not as we hear lectures in the history of Western civilization, but more as we hear sermons. We do not mine this material for archaeological facts. We try to place ourselves so that we can hear its claims and then determine the degree to which they claim us.

Third, the changes that the author of Luke makes in the sources when weaving them into the narrative, as well the changes in the Acts between the Alexandrian and Western versions, remind us again of the permeating role of interpretation in our thinking about God. We need always to evaluate the degree to which our interpretations enhance the witness of the church or detract from it.

The Situation of the Congregation

Luke does not describe the situation of the congregation in a direct way. However, most scholars think that we can recover some aspects of the context from ways in which Luke handles important concerns. As I have already indicated, Luke encourages the community to think that the Hellenistic world is its home and its mission field.

Some previous scholars have thought that Luke's main purpose was to defend the Christian community to the Roman government by assuring civil officials that the early church was not a political threat. However, few interpreters today subscribe to this view. Most academics think that Luke and Acts were prepared originally for the Christian community, not for government officials or other outsiders.

While these materials were not intended to be a manifesto, the careful listener can hear in them the suggestion that the community needs to make its way through the current political situation in such a way as to avoid unnecessary conflict and take advantage of opportunities afforded by political authorities while recognizing the relativity, idolatry, and brokenness of the Roman system. Indeed, the Roman political world will be judged.

Jesus and the apostles were Jewish, and the earliest Christians in Acts lived as faithful Jewish people. They understood themselves to be continuing the story of the God of Israel. Because of their intimate ties with Judaism, we should probably call them Christian Jews.

On the other hand, both Luke and Acts depict repeated and intense acrimony between some (not all) Jewish leaders and Jesus and the early church (e.g., Lk. 5:29–6:11; 12:1–11; 13:10–17; Acts 3:1–4:22; 5:17–42; 6:8–8:1). While some authentic memories of disagreement probably lie behind these materials, debate was characteristic of first-century Judaism. Today's scholarly consensus is that the present form of this material reflects conflict between selected Jewish people and the church in Luke's time.

As I explain in chapter 8, the church and Judaism dispute the degree to which the church is an authentic expression of Judaism, especially in light of the Gentile mission. (The church invited Gentiles into companionship with the God of Israel without fully initiating the converts into Judaism.) The Lukan church retrojected aspects of this tension into the narratives of Jesus and the early church.

Relationships within the Lukan community also contribute elements of tension to the context. Many scholars think that Luke and Acts presume a setting in which Christian Jews and

Gentile Christians are exploring how to practice hospitality toward each other. Should aspects of Judaism be required for all in the church? Ought Christian Jews continue some customs, while not requiring all customs of Gentile Christians?

Jesus stresses that discipleship means taking the way of the cross. Acts portrays many of the social difficulties faced by early Christians. These phenomena prompt many interpreters to conclude that the Lukan church is suffering (e.g., Lk. 8:23–27; 12:49–56; 21:7–24; Acts 4:1–22; 5:17–42; 6:8–8:1). Such difficulty may be connected to the widespread discomfort in Judaism after the destruction of the temple. It could involve pain resulting from discipline carried out by the synagogue and interpreted as persecution.

Other tensions in Luke's context may include the role of women in the Christian community, the use of material resources, how to discern the divine leading, the exercise of authority in the church, false teaching, how to understand the return of Jesus in glory, how to pray, and the relationship of the Christian movement to other philosophies and religions.

The Genre of Luke–Acts

Formal communicators in the ancient world (orators, authors) usually used conventional forms. Each genre had its own style and purpose. Because Luke and Acts are a narrative unity, it follows that they are two parts of one genre. I follow Luke Timothy Johnson in regarding these books as an apology in narrative.[1]

In antiquity, an apology justified a particular interpretation of life. We often think of an apology as making a defense to those outside a community. However, apologies could have an internal focus. When directed to those within the community, an apology was designed to strengthen the community's sense of identity and purpose.[2]

Luke and the Acts are apologies in the latter sense. Luke Timothy Johnson points out, "To a possible outside Hellenistic reader, the Christian movement is presented as a philosophically enlightened, politically harmless, socially benevolent and philanthropic fellowship. But its more immediate purpose is to interpret the Gospel for insiders within the context of a pluralistic environment of both Jews and Gentiles."[3] The Christian community of Luke's day is to understand its mission to be that of enacting in its later time the identity and purpose revealed in Luke–Acts. In the form of story, Luke–Acts offers the listeners a normative interpretation of Jesus Christ and the early church in order to reinforce the community's identity. These materials create a memory of the past of Jesus and the church that can empower the community's identity and behavior in the present.

Many congregations in the long-established denominations would benefit from preaching with the kind of apologetic focus that is found in Luke–Acts. The relationship of today's church to our culture is increasingly like that of the Lukan community: a church that is a minority presence in a wider culture. Furthermore, many of our congregations have a dissipated sense of identity and mission. Preaching with an apologetic quality is especially welcome in the face of the challenges and opportunities of postmodern pluralism and relativism.

The Key Role of the First Testament

The First Testament (a.k.a. Old Testament, Hebrew Bible, Prime Testament) plays a role in the interpretation of Luke–Acts. Luke makes use of a version of the First Testament known as the Septuagint. The Septuagint is a translation of the Hebrew Bible into Greek. Translation from one language to another always involves interpretation. The Septuagint, made in Alexandria, is intended to help the Jewish people in the diaspora maintain Jewish identity while being able to live and move in a Hellenistic setting. (The "Jewish diaspora" refers to Jewish people living outside of Palestine, usually in cultures deeply influenced by Greek thought and customs.) The Septuagint frequently brings out points of positive contact between Jewish and Hellenistic culture. One of my colleagues refers to the Septuagint as "Gentile-friendly."

Throughout Luke–Acts, the author writes with phrases, citations, allusions, and other stylistic features of the Septuagint. Scholars refer to these qualities as Septuagintalisms.

In a general way, the Septuagintal style leads the listener to hear Luke–Acts as continuing the story that is told in the Hebrew Bible and retold (with interpretation) in the Septuagint. Listeners are to recognize that the work of the God of Israel is now expanded in a fresh way into the Gentile world by means of Jesus Christ and the church.

In addition, many of the references to the Septuagint are quite specific. They echo particular passages, stories, ideas, images, and feelings from the Septuagint. Frequently the material in Luke–Acts re-presents or re-frames aspects of the Septuagintal references through the story of Jesus and the early church. Echoes of the stories of Elijah and Elisha, for instance, encourage us to recognize that Jesus and the early church move in the prophetic tradition.

Awareness of Septuagintal motifs enriches our understanding of the material written by Luke. Consequently, when working on a passage or theme in Luke or Acts, the preacher should always probe for background in the First Testament. Furthermore, Luke's profound respect for the First Testament can prompt today's preacher and congregation to remember that we, too, need to be immersed in that Testament in order to have a fully biblical picture of God and the divine purposes. A church that treats the First Testament as second-class commits again the heresy of Marcion.

The Faithfulness of God as Foundational Theological Perspective

The foundational theological conviction of Luke–Acts is the faithfulness of God. The two books confirm that God will be faithful to the Lukan community (and to the world) in the same ways that God was faithful to Israel, to Jesus Christ, and to the earliest church. Indeed, as we will see, Luke believes God promises to be faithful to the universal human community. Beyond difficulties in immediate circumstances, God is trustworthy.

This faithfulness is demonstrated through the fresh manifestation of the realm of God (NRSV: kingdom of God) through the ministries of Jesus and the early Christian community. This reign will achieve complete and universal manifestation when Jesus returns. This motif is more fully discussed in chapter 3.

While Luke acknowledges that the realm of God is revealed afresh through Christ and the church, Luke recognizes the divine presence and activity in all times and places (e.g., Lk. 6:35;

Acts 14:17). People who are neither Jewish nor Christian can know something of God (e.g., Lk. 4:25–27; 10:29–37; 23:47; Acts 8:26–40; 16:11–15). This attitude is consistent with the First Testament's confession that the divine presence is universal (e.g., Ex. 15:11; Deut. 10:17–18; 1 Kings 8:41–43; 2 Kings 5:1–19; Ps. 47:2; Dan. 2:47; Wis. 5:18; Sir. 35:15–16).

The motif of divine faithfulness is crucial for the preacher today. Many contemporary congregations in the long-established denominations are beleaguered. We look at our declining memberships and declining real dollars for mission and wonder if we can survive. We try to carry on theological conversation but often do little more than parrot the latest ideas from talk shows. We struggle with tension around race, gender, and sexual orientation. Our churches need to grow in the knowledge that God is faithful. Such awareness will both help relieve our anxiety and help us testify with the boldness depicted of the disciples in Acts.

CHAPTER 2

Preaching from Luke–Acts

The preacher attempts to help the congregation name and respond to the divine presence and leading in the contemporary world. To use a Lukan image, a sermon is a journey of conversation whose goal is to interpret life from the perspective of the realm of God. The conversational journey includes the witness of the Bible, the preacher, the Christian community and the wider world, and theological norms and methods.[1] The sermon is not, in this view, an out-loud give-and-take between preacher and congregation, but is typically a monologue with the quality of conversation.

In this chapter I explore some practical approaches to facilitating this conversation in connection with Luke–Acts. The chapter first summarizes a method that helps us with the essential task of the preacher: to engage Luke's witness theologically. I turn to the hermeneutic of analogy as a frequently fruitful partner in the conversation when preaching. The heart of the chapter focuses on preaching on *themes* in Luke–Acts. I recall the importance, stressed in chapter 1, of bringing the First Testament into the sermon as frequently as possible. The chapter concludes with possibilities for sermon series on themes in Luke–Acts and reflects briefly on these writings in the Revised Common Lectionary.

A Clear Theological Method

A clear theological method is the most important component for preaching from Luke–Acts. Through exegesis the preacher clarifies the witness of a theme or passage. What does Luke ask us to believe to be true? The pastor and congregation then need to assess the relationship of that claim to the core of Christian conviction that transcends the particular witness of Luke, Acts, or other particular biblical writings. The character of that relationship will help determine the purpose of the sermon. Toward this end, I now summarize a method, occasionally employed in chapters 3–7, to help identify that relationship.[2]

1. Is the witness of the theme or text appropriate to the core of Christian conviction?[3] The core of Christian conviction is the news that God promises unconditional love to each and all and that God perpetually wills justice for each and all. In this frame of reference, justice refers to relationships of love. A just community is one in which all relationships mediate love. The core of Christian conviction, then, is an ellipse with two centers: unconditional love and an unrelenting will for justice. All things in the Christian community should be consistent with this center.

   The preacher, then, asks of every theme or passage, "Does this material witness to God's unconditional love for each and all and God's will for justice for each and all?"

2. Is the witness of the theme or text intelligible? In order to converse with a theme or text in preaching, we need to be able to make sense of it in three ways.

   (a) Can we plainly understand the claims of the theme or text? The preacher and the congregation need to be able to get the point(s).

   (b) Is the witness of the theme or text logically consistent within itself and with other beliefs, actions, and feelings in the Christian community? In particular, are the claims of the text coherent with the promise of God's unconditional love for all and God's universal call for justice? If claims in the Christian community contradict one another, the credibility of Christian witness is called into question.

(c) Can we *believe* the witness of the theme or text? Yale theologian David Kelsey says that Christian claims must be "seriously imaginable" within a culture.[4] That is, we should be able to envision the claims of the text actually taking place in the world, given the ways in which we understand the cosmos and the divine relationship to it. However, this criterion must be handled delicately. Some themes and passages rightly ask us to enlarge our vision of what is possible.

This subcriterion is further complicated by the fact that we can sometimes distinguish between the surface witness of a theme or text and its deeper witness. This distinction is often helpful when dealing with surface witness as the simple claim of the text in its cultural expression and worldview. The deeper dimension of the text is the dimension of the claim of the text that transcends the particular worldview in which it is cast. For instance, Luke tells the story of Jesus' multiplying a handful of fish and bread to feed five thousand people (Lk. 9:10–17). At the surface level, the witness of this is not seriously imaginable. However, at the deeper level, the passage testifies to divine providence even in the wilderness experiences of life. The latter claim is more than seriously imaginable; it is essential for Christian identity.

3. Is the witness of the theme or text morally plausible? Closely related to the norm of appropriateness to the core of Christian conviction, this criterion calls for the moral treatment of all, that is, for all to be able to experience divine unconditional love and justice. From time to time, the church encounters a theme or passage that denies God's unconditional love or justice to a person, a group, or an element of nature. In that case, the preacher needs to help explain why the claim of that theme or text is not acceptable in the Christian household.

Using these criteria, a preacher can usually identify one of the following relationships that should exist between the congregation and the theme or text.

When a theme or text is appropriate to the core of Christian conviction, intelligible, and morally plausible, the preacher and congregation can altogether agree with it. The preacher explains the claims of the motif or passage and draws out their implications for today's Christian community and world.

The preacher and congregation may agree with part of the witness of the motif or passage and disagree with other parts. For instance, a text may be appropriate to the core of Christian conviction and morally plausible, but unintelligible at the surface level. Upon further reflection, the pastor determines that the text is intelligible in its deeper dimensions. The sermon, then, needs to help the congregation make such a movement in its own thinking.

When a theme or passage is inappropriate to the core of Christian conviction, unintelligible on any level, or morally implausible, the minister is called to disagree with it. The sermon can help the congregation understand the claim of the biblical material and why that claim is not welcome in the Christian household. In addition, the sermon should go beyond critiquing the motif or passage by helping the congregation recognize how the core of the Christian message views the matter under consideration. For instance, if a text denies God's love to someone, the sermon needs to encourage the congregation to recognize how the core of the Christian message asserts divine love for that very person.

A preacher can ignore a theme or a passage. However, I do not recommend this alternative, even when the claims of the biblical material are theologically difficult. Material that is ignored is still available to the congregation in the Bible. Some Christians will find it and make use of it. They may interpret it idiosyncratically or even dangerously. Every theme or text can become an occasion for positive Christian teaching, even when the preacher must help the congregation disagree with aspects of the passage or theme.

Hermeneutic of Analogy

A theme or text that is appropriate to the core of Christian conviction, intelligible, and morally plausible sometimes speaks directly to the contemporary world. For instance, we are sinners in need of the awareness of grace.

Sometimes, however, the significance(s) of an appropriate, intelligible, and morally plausible motif or passage for today's world is not immediately evident. The text may refer to issues that are no longer alive or make cultural assumptions that we no longer share. For instance, few people in the long-established denominations believe that the world is occupied by personal beings called demons. At such times, preachers can frequently make use of the hermeneutic of analogy.[5]

This hermeneutic presumes both similarities and dissimilarities between antiquity and the world of today. Many elements of Luke's world are dissimilar to our setting (e.g., we wear different kinds of clothing; we eat different foods; we work at different jobs; we speak different languages). While these cultural forms differ, similarities of experience often transcend the specific differences. For instance, although few people today believe in personal beings called demons, we can identify many situations in which individuals and communities are negatively affected by forces outside themselves in ways that are analogous to demon possession in the world of antiquity. The names differ but the experience of restriction of life is similar. Hence a preacher can frequently ask, "Are the setting, characters, events, and values in the theme or text similar to situations, persons, groups, events, or other experiences in our setting?"

One aspect of the hermeneutic of analogy deserves special comment. As previously observed, the author of Luke–Acts sometimes portrays Jewish people in a negative way. They criticize and crucify Jesus. They criticize and harass the church. They kill Stephen and send Paul on the path toward death. The preacher can make analogies between their negative qualities and the contemporary church. "How similar we are to the Pharisees in our text!"

However, I caution against simplistic use of this analogy. As noted in the preceding chapter, the negative portrayal of Jewish people in Luke–Acts often moves in the direction of caricature. Caricature bears false witness against the neighbor (see Ex. 20:16). Furthermore, the preacher who makes a negative analogy between the Jewish people of antiquity and

Christians of today contributes to the anti-Semitism that is still potent in today's world. The preacher needs to criticize this portrayal of the Jewish people as inappropriate to the core of Christian conviction and morally implausible.

The preacher who needs to critique the thoughts, feelings, and actions of today's church can often do so by finding analogies between the disciples and the early church in Luke–Acts. While these figures sometimes make positive demonstrations of faith and actions, they also sometimes misunderstand, misbelieve, and misbehave. They can often serve the preacher as negative analogies. For example, when confronted with the need to feed five thousand people in the wilderness, the Twelve initially exclaim that they do not have the resources (Lk. 9:10–17). How do we make a similar exclamation? At first the believers in Jerusalem do not welcome Paul as a follower of Jesus. They are suspicious (Acts 9:26). How are we likewise suspicious? Apollos had received John's baptism and was highly intelligent, but had an inadequate understanding of the manifestation of the rule of God through Jesus. Hence, Priscilla and Aquila "took him aside and explained the Way of God to him more accurately" (Acts 18:26b). How are we today like Apollos?

Preaching Themes in Luke–Acts

The purpose of biblical preaching is to interpret the significance of an aspect of the biblical witness for the church and world today. In the broad sense, the biblical preacher does for the contemporary church what the authors and preachers in the biblical period did for communities of faith in antiquity: identify the presence and leading of God with the help of sacred traditions. The Bible is a lens (or better, a series of lenses) through which to view the divine intentions for the world. Most biblical preaching today focuses on individual passages in the Bible, for example, the parable of the widow and the unjust judge (Lk. 19:1–8).

Biblical preaching can also focus on *themes* in the Bible.[6] My use of "theme" is not a formal classification in contemporary biblical scholarship. By theme, I speak informally of ideas, images, associations, expressions, practices, values, or behaviors that develop across a body of biblical literature. A preacher can sometimes focus on a theme in a specific biblical book. For instance, forgiveness is such a motif in the gospel of Matthew. Themes can span several books, either from the hand of a single author or from several authors. In this vein, the preacher could trace "salvation by grace through faith" through the writings of Paul. Obedience and disobedience are themes in materials influenced by Deuteronomic theology. A preacher can follow some themes across the whole Bible. For instance, the character and effects of sin, as well as the divine response, occupy much of the Bible from Genesis through Revelation.

Preaching from individual passages and preaching from themes partake of a reciprocal relationship. The minister who preaches on a particular passage should always set that passage in its literary context. By doing so, the preacher will nearly always find connections between the passage and other parts of the document of which it is a part and larger patterns in the Bible. While this pastor gives primary attention to the individual text, that attention is informed by echoes and connections from elsewhere. A sensitive preacher takes account of larger thematic patterns when developing a sermon on a single passage.

Likewise, when preaching from a theme, a minister examines individual passages to determine the contribution of each passage to the theme. The exegesis of a particular passage does not control the shaping of the sermon as it does when the pastor preaches from a single text. But the exegesis of particular passages helps the preacher understand how particular passages enrich the development of the theme.

As noted previously, Luke and Acts constitute a literary world. The author introduces themes in Luke and subsequently develops them in Luke and Acts. We can fully understand the significance of a theme in these books only by tracing that theme from Luke through Acts. When we focus only on an isolated text and do not take into account the larger pattern of development, we can badly distort the intent of the text. For instance, in the Sermon on the Plain the author of Luke quotes Jesus as saying harshly, "Woe to you who are rich, for you have received your consolation" (Lk. 6:24). The term "woe" in this context (influenced by apocalypticism) indicates eternal condemnation. This passage by itself suggests that while the wealthy may now revel in luxury, they will suffer in the age to come. Later material in Luke–Acts modifies this viewpoint. The wealthy can be welcomed into the reign of God when they repent of hoarding wealth at the expense of others and when they put their resources at the service of the community in order to provide for all.

Chapters 3–7 each focus on a different theme in Luke–Acts: the reign of God, the Holy Spirit, the great reunion of the human family, the restoration of women in the realm of God, and Lukan perspectives on material resources.

When preparing to preach on a theme, a pastor engages in exegesis much as when preparing to preach from a passage, but with some modifications to account for the wider concern of preaching from a theme.

- There is no substitute for reading Luke–Acts over and over in order for the story to soak into our bones. Indeed, in recent years the biblical storytelling movement points out that *hearing* biblical materials read aloud often helps us develop fresh sensitivities.[7] We develop great empathy for the narrative world. We begin to see connections between parts of the story that we may not have seen previously. We often develop intuition for relationships among texts that we have not noticed before. We develop a feel for the text so that when we read a passage we sense its place in the larger narrative world.

- Listeners in antiquity heard words, images, and themes with preassociations from Judaism or from the wider Hellenistic environment. As much as possible, the preacher needs to discover these associations. Bible dictionaries will often provide valuable information about the backgrounds of the theme. The interpreter can then assess the degree to which Luke (or another biblical writer) drew upon that background directly or modified it. When working with Luke–Acts, we need to pay particular attention to background materials in the First Testament and in the literature of Judaism in the period of the second temple, especially apocalypticism.

Knowledge of Hellenistic religious and cultural assumptions is also useful, especially when working with Acts. What do listeners bring with them to the theme? How does the author invite them to relate to these preassociations? Are they confirmed? Enlarged or refined? Reshaped? Corrected? The minister eventually needs to decide how much of this background material to include in the sermon.

- We need to learn how to recognize the theme in Luke–Acts. Much of this identification will result from the intuitive sympathies that develop from reading and hearing the text repeatedly. What are the key words, images, ideas, actions, and values that signal the presence and development of the theme? A concordance and Bible dictionaries will often alert us to the whereabouts of the theme. However, a preacher can seldom prepare for preaching on a theme by doing nothing more than reading an article on a key word in a Bible dictionary. The study of a theme is usually more than the study of a single word.

- We need to identify key passages in Luke–Acts that introduce and develop the theme. The preacher conducts a mini-exegesis of each contributing passage. Time will not permit a full-scale historical-critical and literary-critical encounter with every text that manifests the theme, but a minister can consider elements of the passage that particularly point toward the development of the theme. How does each passage enlarge our understanding of the theme? Reading the commentaries on each passage is crucial for developing a detailed acquaintance with each text. However, the preacher cannot assume that the commentaries will reveal all that the preacher needs to know about a theme. The commentaries sometimes consider passages atomistically, that is, as self-contained units, without paying attention to wider connections. Because the preacher needs to interact with commentaries on a number of passages, the preacher probably needs to budget more time for working with the commentaries on a thematic sermon than when basing a sermon on a single text.

- Many preachers find it helpful to summarize the major claim of the theme in a sentence or a short paragraph. What does Luke–Acts ask us to believe to be true of this theme? While the depth and complexity of a theme can never be satisfactorily reduced to a propositional summary, such a statement helps the preacher develop a clear understanding of the central claim of the text and engage the text with the theological method articulated above.

- The sermon will likely need to discuss several of the passages in which the theme appears. Which ones should the preacher select as most important to be mentioned in the sermon?

- The preacher needs to decide whether a single sermon can do justice to a theme, or whether the theme should be spread over a series of sermons. If the latter, the preacher needs to identify an organizational principle by which to plan the different sermons. For examples of such patterns, see page 28, "Developing a Sermon Series."

- Themes in some biblical documents are in dialogue with themes (or texts) in other documents. When the canon contains perspectives that differ, or even contradict one another, the preacher should usually bring this material into the sermon so that the congregation can become part of a conversation that seeks to sort out which perspectives are more or less adequate for today's community. A single sermon cannot always deal fully with such questions, but it can at least introduce them to the table of conversation.

After determining the hermeneutical relationship between the theme and the congregation, the preacher needs to determine how to organize the sermon so that it will have a good chance of engaging the congregation in meaningful conversation about the significance of the theme for the contemporary church and world. The hermeneutic of analogy is often a direct partner as the preacher seeks to find similarities between the setting and purpose of the theme in antiquity and its meaning for today.

The First Testament and Luke–Acts

In chapter 1, I noted that the Lukan author assumes the First Testament as background for understanding Luke–Acts. Many words, images, ideas, characters, turns of plot, and events in Luke–Acts resonate with the First Testament. When we hear these things, we remember their associations in the First Testament and we interpret Luke–Acts from their perspective. For example, John the Baptist preaches in the wilderness from Isaiah 40, the beginning of a great poem of consolation for the Jewish people in exile in Babylonia. When we hear Isaiah's words in Luke, we recognize that faithful people are again in a kind of exile by virtue of living in the old, corrupt age of history. However, we can live in hope because, as God returned the exiles to their homeland, so the universal sovereign will regenerate this world, and "all flesh shall see the salvation of God" (Lk. 3:6).

Furthermore, Luke regards the story of Jesus and the church as an extension of the story of Israel. Through Jesus Christ and the church, God is continuing the story begun in the First Testament. The community can have confidence that God will bring this story to its completion because God has proven faithful to the Jewish community in the earlier chapters of the narrative (i.e., the First Testament). For instance, the Lukan author tells three stories in Acts of the deliverance of early Christian witnesses from prison (Acts 5:17–21; 12:6–11; 16:23–29). Listeners whose ears are attuned to the First Testament resonate with the story of the deliverance of Israel from slavery in Egypt. Just as God led the Hebrew slaves from bondage into freedom, so God is now leading the early Christian community through its periods of difficulty into freedom.

Because material from the First Testament is so important for understanding Luke–Acts, the preacher should help the congregation hear the resonance between the First Testament and themes and texts in the Lukan volumes. The minister will usually need to summarize the material that the Lukan author presumes from the First Testament. Given the biblical illiteracy of many congregations today, a preacher cannot casually mention a story or detail that the author presupposes the first-century congregation would know.

When the time allotted for a sermon will not allow for a summary of such material from the First Testament, the preacher or worship leader might add a brief teaching moment to the reading of the lesson from Luke–Acts. The preacher could then explain the background from the First Testament that is important for hearing the reading from Luke or Acts and the sermon. Indeed, pertinent material from the First Testament could be included as a formal Bible reading in the service of worship.

Developing a Sermon Series on a Theme from Luke–Acts

The preacher can often develop a single sermon on a theme in Luke–Acts that brings the congregation into a satisfactory conversation with the theme. However, the density of some themes calls for more than one sermon. To preach only one sermon on the theme would not allow preacher and congregation to engage the theme sufficiently. Sometimes a theme intersects the circumstances of the congregation in such a vital way that more than one sermon is needed on the theme.

In such situations, a preacher can develop a series of sermons. The first sermon introduces the series. Each succeeding sermon builds on the ones preceding. Such a series allows the preaching conversation to consider the theme and its relationship to the congregation in depth and complexity. A series creates continuity in the pulpit from one week to the next. When such a series is underway, members of the listening community often feel a sense of anticipation from one week to the next.

At the same time, each sermon must communicate a distinct message of its own because many members and friends do not attend worship every week. A few people may hear only one sermon. The preacher can help sporadic attenders to become familiar with the series, and with the place of a particular sermon in the series, by announcing the series in the church newsletter and by summarizing the series (and the focus of each sermon) in the worship bulletin. During the service of worship, the preacher or worship leader can take a moment at the reading of the Bible lesson to outline the series and to indicate the place of the sermon for the day in the unfolding of the series.

Most sermon series last from four to eight weeks. When a series lasts longer than eight weeks, the attention of the congregation often begins to wane.

A series on a theme may be organized in one of at least three ways. (1) The preacher could select a series of passages from Luke–Acts that represent the theme. The first sermon would introduce the theme and the issues that it raises for the congregation and would provide background material from Judaism and other sources, ancient and contemporary. Each subsequent sermon would focus on the particular biblical passage but with an eye toward how that passage enriches the congregation's understanding of the theme. For instance, when preaching on the theme of the Holy Spirit, the preacher might put together a series as follows:

- Sermon 1. This sermon suggests the importance of the theme of the Holy Spirit for the church and sketches the roles of the Holy Spirit in Judaism. It uses Luke 1:26–38 as a model for understanding the overarching work of the Spirit in Luke's writings: Through the Spirit, God manifests the divine rule.

- Sermon 2, Luke 3:21–22. The descent of the Spirit at the baptism of Jesus confirms that Jesus is filled and guided by the Spirit. The ministry of Jesus–witnessing to the manifestation of the reign of God–is a paradigm of the Spirit-filled life.

- Sermon 3, Luke 4:14–30. Jesus details the work of the Spirit by citing a text from Isaiah. The Spirit is at work whenever good news comes to the poor and captives are released. The sermon can illustrate these phenomena from the ministry of Jesus.

- Sermon 4, Acts 2:1–21. The same Spirit that filled and guided Jesus also fills and guides the church. The Spirit constitutes the church as a community of witnesses to the divine reign. The sermon can indicate how the reign of God is embodied in the church, for example, through reversal of the confusion of the human community that took place at Babel.

- Sermon 5, Acts 4:1–22. The Holy Spirit leads the community to witness boldly to the reign of God, even in the face of opposition.

- Sermon 6, Acts 10:1–33. This passage reveals an essential quality of the work of the Spirit: It leads us to enlarge our understanding of God's love and God's will for justice.

- Sermon 7, Acts 15:8–28. The Holy Spirit helps to name the divine presence and leading as the Spirit operates through conversation that takes place in community.

- Sermon 8, Acts 20:17–35. This sermon would focus on Paul's indication that the Spirit is a constant strengthening companion as Paul faces an uncertain future while he returns to Jerusalem to witness to the realm of God. The Spirit is similarly with us.

This approach simplifies one of the preacher's tasks when preaching from a theme: selecting materials for the reading of the Bible during the service of worship.

(2) Each sermon could consider the appearance of the theme in succeeding sections of the narrative. The first sermon would introduce the theme and the issues it presents to the congregation. Each subsequent sermon would consider the unfolding of the theme in the natural divisions of the narrative as demarcated in chapter 3.

For example, a sermon series on the reign of God could unfold as follows:

- Sermon 1. This sermon can indicate the importance of this subject matter for the congregation. The sermon can recall Jewish backgrounds regarding the notion of the reign of God, as well as the foreshadowing of this theme in Luke 1:5–2:52.

- Sermon 2. This sermon, focusing on Luke 3:1–9:50, fills out Luke's understanding of the reign of God as manifested afresh through the ministry of Jesus.

- Sermon 3. Luke 9:51–19:27 uses the motif of the journey to explore the relationship of the disciples of Jesus to the reign of God.
- Sermon 4. This message turns to Luke 19:28–Acts 1:26 to discover the depth of conflict between the reign of God and the rulers of the present age, epitomized in the confrontation in Jerusalem between Jesus and the conventional authorities. The resurrection assures listeners that God has the power to bring the divine realm to fulfillment.
- Sermon 5. The church becomes a community whose life embodies the realm of God in Acts 2:1–8:3 and 8:4–40. However, the church (like Jesus in Luke) experiences conflict with traditional religious leaders concerning this reign.
- Sermon 6. Beginning with the call of Paul and Peter's mission to Cornelius, the community welcomes Gentiles as a sign of great reunion of the human family that is a part of the reign of God (Acts 9:1–28:31).

This approach does not immediately resolve the question of which passages from the Bible to read during the service of worship. The worship planning team can select passages that represent the development of the theme in the segment of the narrative that is the focus for each Sunday. During the service of worship, the Bible reader can alert the congregation to the representative nature of the text.

(3) The series could be organized according to subthemes that are important to the main theme. Many themes contain subthemes that draw their life from the theme but that have particular foci. Subthemes sometimes occur in particular passages. The first sermon could introduce the theme and provide background materials, with each succeeding sermon focusing on a particular subtheme.

For example, a series could be based on the use of material resources (e.g., wealth) from the perspective of the reign of God. The subthemes in this topic develop across the narrative of Luke–Acts.

- Sermon 1. This sermon indicates why it is important for the Christian community to come to a clear understanding of its relationship with material resources and recalls ways that Judaism understood poverty, wealth, and covenantal community.

- Sermon 2. This sermon develops the criticism of the wealthy that is prominent in Luke–Acts.

- Sermon 3. This sermon highlights the divine concern for the poor in Luke–Acts.

- Sermon 4. This sermon helps the congregation recognize that one means whereby God provides for the poor is by inviting the rich to repent of their idolatry of wealth and to put their resources at the disposal of the community. In this way God blesses the poor through the community. God relieves the wealthy of the anxiety of trying to secure their lives by building ever-greater barns.

Like the preceding approach, this does not immediately indicate which texts from the Bible can be read as the lessons during public worship. Again, the pastor and other worship planners might choose texts that represent the relationship between the theme and the subtheme that is the focus for the day. At the time of the Bible reading, the worship leader can indicate the representative relationship between the text and the topic.

Preaching from Luke–Acts in the Revised Common Lectionary

Readings from Luke appear in the Revised Common Lectionary primarily in year C. While the whole of Luke is not appointed, selections are drawn from each chapter and represent Luke's main emphases. Readings from Acts are found mainly in the Sundays of Easter in years A, B, and C.

Pastors normally focus the sermon on the passage for the day. A responsible preacher will consider ways in which the larger themes of Luke–Acts inform the text that is the focus for the day. Beyond that, when a particular text is important to a theme in Luke or Acts, a preacher could easily develop a sermon on that theme. The preacher could use the appearance of the text in the lectionary as a port of entry into the larger theme. After lifting up the theme as the focus of the sermon, the preacher could trace the theme through the Lukan author's two volumes. For instance, the story of the healing of the bent-over woman in Luke 13:10–17 (Proper 16 [21], year C) could lead the preacher to consider the theme of the restoration of women in the reign of God. The outpouring of the Holy Spirit on the Gentiles in Acts 10:44–48 (Easter 6, year B) could open the door to a sermon on the theme of the great reunion of the human family.

The Revised Common Lectionary mishandles Acts in two ways. First, in the Sundays of Easter, the Lectionary drops the primary reading from the First Testament and replaces it with a reading from Acts. (The Psalms are the only voice from the First Testament left in the readings on the Sundays of Easter, and the Psalms are intended to be used responsively.) By making this omission, the lectionary devalues the First Testament by intimating that the First Testament is not necessary for the church. Because the book of Acts is the replacement document, the lectionary subtly leaves the impression that Acts supersedes the First Testament in importance for the church. This situation contributes to the devaluation of the church's Jewish heritage, which results in anti-Judaism and even anti-Semitism. I strongly recommend that the worship planners counteract this development by *adding* passages from the First Testament to the readings for the Sundays of Easter.

Second, while the readings from Acts in the Revised Common Lectionary are fairly representative of the main themes in Acts, the readings are few in number and tell only a part of the story that is contained in Acts. The lectionary appoints *no* passages from Acts 6, 12–15, 18, or 20–28! These omissions are serious. For instance, the pivotal story of the Apostolic Council (Acts 15) is never read. Only a fraction of the narrative of Paul's journeys is heard. The congregation is never exposed in public worship to the part of Acts wherein Paul fulfills the commission that Jesus gave to the church to carry the gospel to the "ends of the earth." The listening community does not follow

Paul from his arrest on the torturous journey to Rome. Consequently, at least in the liturgical setting, the congregation is deprived of the Lukan author's interpretation of Paul.

The preacher and worship leaders can take a couple of actions to help alleviate this situation. For one, when preaching from texts in Luke–Acts in the lectionary, the preacher can trace themes from those passages into the parts of Acts that do not appear in the lectionary. The congregation would thereby get to hear those stories and their place in the unfolding narrative of the early church.

For another, the Revised Common Lectionary provides for reading several books of the Second Testament seriatim, for example, Matthew, Mark, Luke. This approach has the salutary effect of helping the congregation enter the literary and theological worlds of these documents. I recommend that the congregation create a table of readings by which to hear the whole story of Acts. Since Luke is heard in year C, the readings from Acts might come in year A as an additional reading or as a substitute reading each week. The congregation could then follow the narrative from Luke through Acts in successive years. An intriguing alternative derives from the fact that the ministry of Jesus in Luke is a paradigm for the ministry of the church in Acts. On every Sunday of year C, the preacher and worship planners could pair readings from Luke and Acts that correlate a paradigmatic activity or teaching in Luke with passages that show how the church in Acts is shaped by the paradigm. For still another alternative, the worshiping community might replace the Revised Common Lectionary for a year or two with a table of readings that follow the story of Luke–Acts. The planning team could select readings from the First Testament that directly coordinate with motifs in the readings from Luke–Acts.

CHAPTER 3

Preaching on the Realm of God

The realm (NRSV: kingdom) of God is an overarching theme that runs throughout Luke–Acts. We can hear everything that occurs in these two volumes through the notion of the divine reign. Other themes add specificity to this one.

In this chapter I provide an overview of the notion of the realm of God in the stream of Judaism that most directly informs Luke–Acts. The heart of the chapter is an extended exploration of how Luke–Acts develops this notion. The chapter wrestles with how the contemporary church might understand and critically appropriate the notion of the reign of God as refracted through Luke–Acts. The chapter ends with a sermon on the theme.

Preachers and scholars sometimes speak as if the reign of God appears in Jesus Christ for the first time. For instance, I sometimes hear Christians refer to the rule of God "dawning" or "beginning" in Jesus. However, as noted below, from the apocalyptic point of view, God has ruled the universe since its creation. The divine dominion does not come into being for the first time through Jesus Christ, but is only manifest in a fresh way.

I underline this point because Christians sometimes drift into anti-Judaism by posing a sharp, negative contrast between God's ruling activity before and after Jesus Christ. In this pattern of thinking, God was involved in the world prior to Jesus in an inferior way, whereas after Jesus, God has become involved in a way that is brand new and much better. Luke's view is quite different. The event of Jesus Christ signals only that the time line of history is winding toward its conclusion.

The Realm of God in Early Judaism

In antiquity a "kingdom" included place, time, and activity. A monarch ruled a specific place for a specific time. The term "kingdom" (Greek: *basileia*) is sometimes translated as realm, rule, reign, or dominion. The realm of God is God's ruling activity over a particular place at a particular time.

A fundamental tenet of Jewish thinking in the First Testament is that the God of Israel is sovereign over Israel, over other nations, over all aspects of history, and over the entire cosmos (e.g., Ps. 93). Consequently, the Jewish people frequently speak of God as king (monarch, sovereign, ruler). The First Testament and other early Jewish literature sometimes refer to the divine rule as the "kingdom of God." This expression is frequently translated as "reign of God," "rule of God," "realm of God," "dominion of God," and so forth. Some of the rabbis in the period of the second temple speak of God as "Sovereign of the Universe."

The apocalyptic movement, one of the widespread religious movements in Judaism in the first century C.E., infused the notion of "reign of God" with a particular theological content containing a distinctive understanding of the time line of history that is explained below. The Lukan author's primary vision of the reign of God is drawn from this movement. However, neither Luke nor Acts belongs to the genre of apocalypse, nor is Luke a straightforward apocalyptic theologian. The author of Luke–Acts modifies the typical apocalyptic time line at the end of history and supplements the apocalyptic interpretation of history with ideas and images from other strands of Judaism and from ideas that were popular in wider Hellenistic religions and philosophies.

Contemporary Christians in the long-established denominations sometimes look down on apocalyptic thinking because they think of it as pie-in-the-sky. Consequently, it is important to realize that apocalypticism did not arise as escapism. To the contrary, apocalypticism arose in order to help the community make sense of a profound contradiction between experience and tradition. According to the apocalyptic theologians, the God of Jewish tradition promised to bless the world. However, much of human experience since the fall has been marked by brokenness, oppression, and suffering. What is the meaning of the suffering of this present age? And what will God do in order to keep God's promise? Apocalypticism hopes to help the community to witness faithfully while enduring the struggles of the present, and to live in hope. These preachers seek to help the community realize why they can continue to have confidence in a loving and just God in a world so rife with evil.

The seedbed of apocalyptic theology is the prophetic movement in Israel, especially the notion that a day would come when God would appear to judge those who practice idolatry, injustice, and other forms of sin, and to redeem the faithful. While apocalyptic theology is not found in a fully developed form in writings in the First Testament that predate 300 B.C.E., proto-apocalyptic impulses are found in Isaiah 56–66 and in Zechariah 7–12. Daniel 7–12, written about 165 B.C.E., is the only piece of fully developed apocalyptic theology in the First Testament. However, many other Jewish writings from 300 B.C.E. to 200 C.E. have an apocalyptic flavor. These materials include books (not often well known among Christian preachers) such as Enoch, 2 Esdras (4 Ezra), the Testaments of the Twelve Patriarchs, and Baruch. Many Jewish people in the world of the first century who were not complete apocalyptists were nonetheless sympathetic to the basic apocalyptic demarcation of history and anticipated the apocalyptic hope.

The apocalyptic theologians think that the history of the cosmos (the created world) unfolds in four eras.[1]

(1) At the time of creation and immediately thereafter (the garden of Eden), the world was as God intended. It was a world in which all relationships were mutual and supportive. Women and men were equal partners in exercising dominion, that is, in helping all things relate together in the way that God wanted. The world was a genuine community in which each element could be all that it was meant to be and in which all elements encouraged one another. These motifs are important to apocalyptic theologians because the time of creation is the paradigm

for the world after the apocalypse. The cosmos will be recreated. Scholars sometimes say that the end time will be like the beginning time. The author of Luke–Acts refers explicitly to this motif by saying that people should repent in preparation for the "universal restoration that God announced long ago through [the] holy prophets" (Acts 3:21).

(2) The period after the fall through the present is a broken time. After Adam and Eve ate the forbidden fruit, God cursed the world. The communality of Eden gives way to idolatry, sin, injustice, division among peoples, poverty, social disparity, sickness, violence, enmity between humankind and nature, and death. Satan and the demons warp the lives of human beings and nature. This age is ambiguous. It can manifest characteristics of Eden, but the world is seldom the complete community of positive relationality that God wishes.

(3) The apocalypse itself is a historical cataclysm in which God intervenes in the history of the world. God and divine agents (e.g., angels) defeat Satan and the demons. For the Lukan author, the apocalypse climaxes with the return of Jesus in glory. However, aspects of the ministry of Jesus prefigure the apocalypse, especially as Jesus confronts Satan and the demons and restores situations to patterns of relationship and community that recollect Eden. The miracles, for example, are mini-apocalypses in which Jesus (or Jesus' representatives) confronts the brokenness of the old world and demonstrates the power of the divine realm to restore.

Prior to the apocalypse itself a time often called the tribulation will occur. As Satan and the demons perceive that the time of the apocalypse is nearing, they assert their power. As a result, the chaos and violence of the world increase. According to Luke, the early church lives in this period (Lk. 21:5–24). The conflicts experienced by the early Christian community are a part of the struggle of the last days. Luke thinks that the apocalypse itself will be delayed and that this period of struggle will be a long one. The apocolypse itself is dramatic (Lk. 21:25–36).

(4) In the era of the new world, all things will be forever conformed to God's purposes. God's realm will be fully manifested in every relationship and circumstance. This restoration recaptures community as it was in Eden. A noteworthy feature

of this world is that God serves a great banquet to celebrate the end of evil and the full establishment of the divine realm. Aspects of the ministry of Jesus and the early church prefigure aspects of the renewed world. For instance, the resurrection of Jesus is the most dramatic prefiguration of the new age within the realm of the old. Many of Jesus' meals with tax collectors and sinners and the breaking of the bread (the Lukan author's term for the Lord's supper) in the early church anticipate the eschatological banquet.

Luke–Acts: Journey into Awareness of the Realm of God

From Luke 1 through Acts 28, we use our imaginations to follow Jesus and the early Christian communities in a journey discovering how the realm of God is manifested. When we leave Luke–Acts, the narrative of Jesus and the church is a lens through which we interpret today's world.

Luke organizes this literary world around the motif of journey. Echoing a Jewish expression for following God, the early Christian community is called "the Way" (Acts 9:2; 18:25, 26; 19:9, 23; 22:4; 24:14, 22). The listening community in imagination moves not just from one geographical place to another (from Bethlehem through Jerusalem to Rome) but makes a journey of growing theological awareness. We identify empathetically with those who encounter Jesus and with the early church. We experience the realm of God and various modes of responding to it. Eventually the author of Luke–Acts leads us to reflect on the witness that we can make to the realm of God in our own time and place, one that is in continuity with our ancestors in the Acts, in Luke, and in the First Testament.

In Luke–Acts, geographical references, narrative settings, characters, and turns in the plot are often charged with theological meaning. As a basic interpretive procedure, the preacher should ask of each detail, "What does this person, place, or action represent in the narrative?"

The journey falls into ten segments. Each segment has a particular purpose. When preaching from a passage in a particular section, a pastor can take into account the purpose of that section.

Prologue: Luke 1:1–4

The prologue, which is similar to prologues of other works in the time of Luke, develops the intent of this apology.[2] The author of Luke indicates that he has made use of the writing or oral traditions of others but now takes quill in hand so that the listeners will "know the truth." Luke and Acts are designed to assure the listeners that this interpretation of Jesus and the church is reliable.

Luke and Acts are addressed to "Theophilus." In those days wealthy persons sometimes served as benefactors for authors. Perhaps Theophilus was such a person. However, the word Theophilus means "friend" (*philos*) of "God" (*theos*). Consequently, Theophilus may not be an individual but a name that represents all who seek to be companions of God.

The Roots of the Reign of God in Judaism: Luke 1:5—2:52

The Lukan author leaves no doubt that the story of Jesus and the church begins in the First Testament and Judaism. The God of Israel is the God of Jesus Christ and the Christian community. The promises and actions of God through Christ are continuous with the promises and actions of God to Israel. This section prefigures several themes that develop later in Luke and Acts: salvation (i.e., the realm of God) as the goal of Jesus and the Jesus movement, Judaism as the interpretive framework for this story, providing welcome to outcasts and Gentiles, and women as models of faithfulness.

Judaism permeates the atmosphere of Luke 1–2. Angels, agents of God, direct the action. The settings are Jewish. Each human character is faithful to Judaism. Zechariah is a priest. Elizabeth and Zechariah are righteous, that is, living on the basis of the promises and commands of God (Lk. 1:5–24). Mary and Joseph immediately carry out the angel's instructions (1:26–37; 2:1–19). Bethlehem, the birthplace of Jesus, is also the birthplace of David, the preeminent Jewish leader. Mary and Joseph have Jesus circumcised, hence marking Jesus as a member of the Jewish covenantal community (2:21). The parents present Jesus in the temple (2:22–24). Anna and Simeon, prophetess and prophet, indicate that God blesses the birth of Jesus and the life that follows from it (2:25–38). Mary and Joseph make a pilgrimage to Jerusalem at Passover each year (2:41–52). As this part of Luke winds to a close, Jesus, at the age of twelve, articulates the continuity between his ministry and that of Judaism. "Did you not know that I must be about my Father's interests?" (Lk. 2:49, author's trans.).

The speeches in this section are in Septuagintal style. This quality stresses continuity between Judaism and Luke's story. The Magnificat, the famous song of Mary, for example, echoes directly a similar hymn of Hannah when Samuel is born (Lk. 1:46–55; cf. 1 Sam. 2:1–10). The song of Zechariah, popularly known as the Benedictus, is similar to a psalm (Lk. 1:68–79).

The Lukan author carefully frames two themes of promise in this section. By means of Jesus Christ, God will be faithful to the divine promises to preserve the throne of David, that is, to preserve Israel as a people (Lk. 1:32–33, 68–69; cf. 2 Sam. 7:16). However, the author of Luke places this promise within the larger promise that God swore to Sarah and Abraham, the prototypes of Israel (Lk. 1:54–55). The latter pledge is to bless all peoples (Gen. 12:1–3). God keeps faith with Sarah and Abraham by blessing the Gentiles through Jesus Christ. The Gentile blessing is the glory of Israel (Lk. 1:29–32).

This theology of Judaism (a people set apart as a light to the Gentiles), prepares listeners for understanding the later conflict between Jesus (and early Christian Jewish folk) and selected Jewish leaders. When listeners encounter that conflict in the narrative, we realize it is a dialogue that is internal to Judaism regarding the interpretation of the Jewish mission. Jesus engages other Jewish leaders not as an outsider, but as a practicing Jewish person in dispute with other practicing Jewish people regarding what it means to be faithful. This section previews a conflict on the horizon (Lk. 1:34–35).

Jesus Manifests the Realm of God in Galilee: Luke 3:1—9:50

In this section the Lukan author discloses the character of Jesus' ministry: the manifestation of the reign of God in the last days of world history. This disclosure occurs by preaching that announces the realm of God, by gathering a community to witness to it, by teaching that interprets it, and by deeds that express it. Jesus calls twelve associate leaders (whom the author of Luke often calls apostles) and empowers them both to preach the dominion of God and to work signs that express it. This segment also reveals Jewish responses to Jesus ranging from warm embrace to rejection.

Galilee is a significant theological symbol. In the days of Luke, this area was home to a mixed population of Jewish and Gentile folk who had largely congenial relationships. Roughly 100 miles north of Jerusalem, Galilee was on the border between Jewish and Gentile worlds. When Jesus' ministry starts far outside of Jerusalem, the Lukan author makes it clear that Jesus is not beholden to the Jewish religious, political, and economic powers concentrated in conventional Judaism. Indeed, as Luke unfolds, we realize that some conventional Jewish people resist the reign of God. Energy for restoration of the community comes from outside the conventional power structure.

John the Baptist is a prophet who preaches that the last days of world history have arrived (Lk. 3:1–20). Luke thus portrays the ministry of Jesus and the church taking place in the last days. The rest of the story takes place within this eschatological framework. The Baptist quotes Isaiah to demonstrate that the restoration of the world, including the great reunion of Jewish and Gentile families, is now underway in these last days (Lk. 3:4–6).

The baptism of Jesus (a model for the baptism of believers in Acts) assures Jesus and the listening community that the ministry of Jesus and the church takes places at God's gracious call. The baptism shows that the power of the Holy Spirit operates through Jesus (Lk. 3:20–21). God's words at the climax of the short narrative recall Isaiah 42:1 and Psalm 2:7–passages that stress God's intention to bring justice (i.e., right relationship) to the world. The temptation of Jesus indicates both that the Spirit initiates conflict with powers that resist the reign of God and that Jesus is empowered by the Spirit to withstand such conflict (Lk. 4:1–13).

Every scholar known to me regards Luke 4:16–30 as a paradigm that discloses the significance of Jesus and the church for Luke–Acts. As a faithful Jewish leader, Jesus went to the synagogue on the Sabbath. A visiting rabbi was often invited to offer an interpretation of the Bible lessons during the synagogue service. In line with this custom, Jesus reads and interprets Isaiah 61:1–2 (conflated with Isa. 58:6). This short section draws on potent imagery to depict the restoration of the world in the reign of God by means of a series of vivid word pictures. These conditions are not exhaustive, but representative. The good news of abundance for everyone is going out to the poor. God is liberating prisoners and returning sight to the blind. The oppressed are being freed, and the year of God's favor (the eschatological Jubilee) begins.

Luke frequently uses this imagery on two levels: They include both physical conditions and spiritual perception. The blind, for instance, are both those whose eyes are dysfunctional and those who cannot perceive the divine presence and purposes. These images interpret what happens in the ministry of Jesus: The physically blind come to sight even as the spiritually imperceptive come to fresh understanding. They also interpret what happens through the life and witness of the early church in Acts. Not only are the early Christian witnesses agents of the release of prisoners (e.g., the exorcism of persons who are imprisoned by demons), but they are themselves released from prisons in which they have been cast because of their witness.

Jesus becomes the prototype of the Christian preacher by saying, "Today, this scripture has been fulfilled in your hearing." For Jesus interprets the sacred tradition for the sake of helping the community identify God's liberating purposes in the present. The great restoration is underway. In the renewed world, all things will be as God intends.

At first, the crowd welcomes the message. However, they turn on Jesus when the preacher indicates that the restoration will include Gentiles and others outside the conventional Jewish community. Elijah provided food for a Gentile widow in Zarephath (1 Kings 17:1–6). Elisha healed Namaan, not only a Gentile but also a general in the Syrian army, an occasional enemy of Israel (2 Kings 5:1–19). The congregation in the syna-gogue prefigures some responses to Jesus and the church when they attempt to kill Jesus. However, just as God saved Israel by leading the Jews through the Red Sea, so God leads Jesus through the violent mob.

We see this pattern repeatedly in Luke–Acts. Jesus or early Christians proclaim and embody the restoration. Some folk embrace it. Others turn away. Yet God always provides for those who act in trust.

Jesus then calls the first disciples to form the community that witnesses to the divine reign (Lk. 5:1–11). The twelve apostles (Lk. 5:1–11, 27–28; 6:12–16) recall the twelve tribes of Israel. The number twelve does not symbolize the replacement of Israel by the church, but the union of the church with the purpose of Israel to witness to the reign of God for the sake of the blessing of the world. The number twelve signals that the eschatological fulfillment is now underway.

The Lukan author uses the term *apostles* to specify the circle of the Twelve. The broader spectrum of Jesus' followers is of-ten designated *disciples* (though the Twelve are sometimes in-cluded in the disciples). The apostles witness to the divine rule much as Jesus does. Jesus teaches them the ways of the reign of God (e.g., Lk. 9:23–27; 9:51–19:27). The Lukan author thus prepares listeners to pay attention to the Twelve and their suc-cessors as authoritative voices in the author's own church.

Almost immediately, Jesus enters into conflict with some of the leaders of Judaism regarding the divine rule (Lk. 6:1–17) when he interprets the reign of God in the sermon on the plain (6:17–49). This sermon explains the nature of the divine rule and how to live in response to it so that personal and commu-nal life are restored. For instance, Jesus says, "Love your en-emies, do good to those who hate you." This collection is not an exhaustive description of how Jesus' followers are to live, but are focal instances of ways the divine rule shapes attitudes and actions. By noticing how the restoration works in these illustrations, the disciples can imagine how to live the restora-tion in other specific situations.

Jesus then demonstrates the reign of God through several miracles and other encounters (Lk. 7:1–9:18; 9:37–43).

A miracle is a mini-occurrence of the reign of God because the miracle demonstrates the restoration that God plans for all things. Jesus' return in glory will be accompanied by a cosmic miracle in which all things are restored. The miracle stories in Luke model miracle-working for the Christian community in Acts.

Luke 9:18–27 is a fulcrum passage. Some Jewish people in Luke's day believed that a Messiah would be an important agent in revealing the divine rule. (Other Jewish groups did not share that view.) Jesus performs this role in Luke–Acts. According to Luke 9:21–27 the Messiah will be crucified as part of the coming of the divine rule. Indeed, this suffering (the cross, 9:21–22) is an archetype for the lives of Jesus' followers who must bear their crosses daily (9:23–27). The voice of God on the Mount of Transfiguration confirms that God works through such suffering (9:28–36). A significant strand of Jewish tradition had long believed that suffering would often be part of faithful witness (e.g., Isa. 52:13–53:12; 4 Macc. 6:1–7:23; 8:1–18:5, especially 17:17–22). Indeed, the prophets suffered (e.g., Lk. 6:22–26; 11:45–52; 13:33–34; Acts 7:52). Apocalyptic thinkers of Luke's day anticipated a time of suffering (known as the tribulation) in conjunction with the transformation of the old age into the new because the principalities and the powers (i.e., Satan and the demons) would try to prevent the divine reign from coming. However, God proves faithful to Jesus by raising the Savior from the dead. Likewise, the early Christian witnesses in Acts and the Christians of Luke's day can act faithfully even in the face of deadly opposition in the confidence that God is trustworthy.

The Witness to the Realm Journeys to Jerusalem: Luke 9:51—19:27

In this long segment, Jesus and the apostles journey from Galilee to Jerusalem. The journey motif is more than a geographical designation; it is a Lukan image of the life of discipleship. This section is a foreshadowing of the journey of witness that the church in Acts will take as it makes its way toward the complete manifestation of the divine rule. The events and teachings in this section help prepare the church for that later journey. This section broadens the theological interpretation of Jesus and the early Christian mission. Tension heightens between Jesus and some conventional Jewish authorities.

After Jesus sets this journey decisively in motion (Lk. 9:51–62), listeners discover that Jesus empowers the apostles (and other witnesses) to announce and interpret the reign of God and to work its signs and wonders. These followers need more teaching about the divine rule (10:1–23). Some scholars think many of Jesus' words and actions in this part of the gospel are aimed at encouraging a dispirited congregation (e.g., 9:57–62; 11:1–13; 13:6–9; 16:10–13; 17:1–10; 18:1–9; 19:11–27).

The Lukan Jesus tells the most famous of the Lukan parables in this way. Several of the parables are prompted by comments or actions by conventional Jewish leaders. In Luke, a parable is a short narrative that interprets an aspect of the rule of God. Listeners enter the literary world of the parable and experience the world from its point of view. We emerge from the parable looking at our everyday world through its perspective. The meaning of a parable cannot be fully articulated in a proposition. The experience of hearing the story is part and parcel of its meaning. The parable of the good Samaritan, for instance, surprises hearers with the recognition that Samaritans can not only serve the realm of God but act as models of it (Lk. 10:25–37). In the very next passage, we see the realm of God in action as the rabbi Jesus offers the same level of instruction regarding the divine rule to Mary and Martha as he does to males (10:38–42) and teaches the disciples to pray for the final manifestation of that reign (11:1–13).

When Jesus embodies the divine rule by casting out demons, local authorities protest that his exorcising power derives from Satan (Lk. 11:14–27). This controversy becomes the occasion for an extended denunciation of the lack of understanding on the part of the traditional community leaders and a potent exhortation to faithful testimony. Jesus' long discourse climaxes with the claim that the time for the apocalyptic judgment is coming soon. However, Luke's listeners still have time to take the essential step in preparing for it: repentance (11:29–13:9).

The realm of God, demonstrated in the healing of the bent-over woman, is growing in the world through the ministry of

Jesus and the church much like the mustard seed sown in the garden and the yeast mixed into the dough to make bread (Lk. 13:10–21). People who recognize the presence of God's dominion are welcomed into it (13:22–29), while those who do not recognize it will suffer (13:31–35).

One of the most striking features of the journey (and one that reappears prominently in Acts) is table companionship. Many Jewish people believed that after the realm of God had become completely manifest God would serve a great banquet in celebration. For the author of Luke, the reign of God includes the ingathering of tax collectors, sinners, the poor, and others from the margins of conventional society. Jesus' meals anticipate the eschatological celebration (Lk. 14:1–35). When some Jewish leaders protest that tax collectors and sinners should not be welcomed into God's reign, Jesus defends their place at the table by telling the parables of the lost sheep, the lost coin, and the lost children (Lk. 15:1–32).

Those who protest the inclusion of the poor and others in the community under the divine aegis are like the dishonest manager. When these enemies of Jesus choose to serve wealth (and other false gods), they choose to live outside God's rule, and they bring judgment on themselves (Lk. 16:1–18). However, Jesus tells the parable of the rich person and Lazarus as a pastoral warning. The wealthy and others who object to the manifestation of God's reign through Jesus can still repent and join the movement toward the divine rule (16:19–31).

Jesus stresses again that one must repent and faithfully live from the perspective of the divine realm or face the consequences of judgment (Lk. 17:1–10, 20–37; 18:9–14). God can be counted on to bring this reign (18:1–8). Samaritans and children model those who are most receptive to the new world (17: 11–19; 18:15–17), though even the rich can enter it if they renounce their wealth.

In this section of his gospel, the Lukan author repeatedly recalls the emphasis of 9:18–27 that the crucifixion of Jesus plays an important role in the manifestation of the divine rule (e.g., 18:31–34). However, those who recognize the relationship between Jesus' death, the suffering of the church, and the reign of God are like the blind beggar who is given sight (18:35–42). They recognize the remarkable transformations that occur when people embrace the dominion of God as demonstrated by Jesus and that are represented by the conversion of the Zacchaeus, a chief tax collector (19:1–10). The parable of the pounds reminds the listeners that they must continue to increase their witness to the divine reign even as they await its final manifestation (19:11–27).

Confrontation at Jerusalem: Luke 19:28—Acts 1:26

The narrative unit of this part of the plot spans Luke 19:29–Acts 1:26. The developments in Acts 1:1–26 directly continue the events launched in Luke 19:29ff.

Jerusalem, a primary symbol for revelation in Luke and Acts, is the site of this part of the story. The events at Jerusalem demonstrate the power of God to manifest the divine rule even in the face of the most entrenched opposition. This segment also exposes the flaws in the character of the leadership of Judaism and Rome. The cross and the resurrection unmask their pretensions to power. The faithfulness of God is vindicated.

The crowd in Jerusalem welcomes Jesus as they would welcome royalty when they lay their cloaks on the road (Lk. 19:29–40; 2 Kings 9:13). However, the crowd does not wave branches as they do in the other gospels (Mt. 21:8; Mk. 11:8; Jn. 12:13). Luke omits the branches, associated in the Jewish memory of the Maccabean revolt with military victory (2 Macc. 10:1–9). The author of Luke thereby communicates that Jesus is not a military revolutionary. As the story unfolds, we realize that Jesus is altogether innocent of the charges that are leveled against him. Our sense of injustice at the death of Jesus intensifies.

Speaking in ways that would have reminded first-century listeners of the prophets of Israel, Jesus announces the destruction of Jerusalem (Lk. 19:41–44). Jesus does not "cleanse" the temple by overturning the tables of the moneychangers, but engages in a traditional prophetic practice of symbolizing a message, in this case, the destruction of the temple. The destruction of the temple is part of the suffering prior to the complete installation of God's reign (Lk. 21:5–36).

Jesus is immediately harassed by Jewish leaders, largely the chief priests and the scribes (Lk. 19:45–20:47). Jesus is betrayed by one of the apostles, thus cautioning the church not to assume that they are faithful simply on the basis of their affiliation with Jesus or the Christian community. In the very shadow of the cross, Jesus' disciples dispute among themselves as to which of them is the greatest (22:24–28). In the garden of Gethsemane, they sleep when Jesus needs them (Lk. 22:45). Peter denies Jesus (Lk. 22:31–34, 54–63).

Luke does not mention the Pharisees in connection with Jesus' death. Perhaps Luke's church lives in the same neighborhood with Pharisees; by omitting their role in the death of Jesus, the author of Luke eases one tension between the church and the Pharisaic synagogue.

Jesus is murdered at Passover, a primary symbol in Judaism of God's intention to liberate and protect the Jewish community. The Lukan author does not make much use of Passover language to make sense of the death of Jesus. However, the coincidence of these events intimates that Jesus' death and resurrection prefigure the eschatological Passover. The Last Supper anticipates the eschatological banquet that honors the fulfillment of the divine rule (Lk. 22:7–23).

Luke accurately represents the distribution of authority in the legal proceedings against Jesus. The Jewish leaders had no authority to crucify. A Roman official must pronounce the death sentence. The chief priests, scribes, and elders act as prosecutors who bring charges to Rome, represented by Pilate.

Luke portrays the Jewish leaders as less pernicious in the death of Jesus than they appear in Matthew and Mark (22:66–71). Luke's account of the proceedings before the Jewish council is far shorter. Whereas Mark and Matthew show the council in repeated violation of its own rules of evidence and procedure, Luke suggests that the council honored some of its own legal precepts. Nevertheless, the prosecutors bring false charges when they say, "We found this [person] perverting our nation, forbidding us to pay taxes to the emperor, and saying that he himself is the Messiah, a king" (Lk. 23:2).

Pilate acknowledges that the charges are false (Lk. 23:3–5). Wanting to be dissociated from these proceedings, Pilate assigns Jesus to Herod (Galilean procurator) who agrees that Jesus is without guilt (Lk. 23:6–12). In legal matters, Jewish custom required the agreement of two witnesses to establish proof. However, in these proceedings involving the death sentence, two witnesses never agree with each other against Jesus. Pilate represents the dry rot within Rome by yielding to the mob's cry, "Crucify him." Jesus dies obediently. "Father, into your hands I commend my spirit" (Lk. 23:46).

Luke does not condemn Judaism as such, nor all its leaders. Indeed, good Joseph of Arimathea (a member of the council and "good and righteous") sees that Jesus was buried according to Jewish prescription. Joseph, representing some other Jewish leaders, "had not agreed to their plan and action" (Lk. 23:50–55).

A group of women make their way to the tomb to anoint Jesus' body on the first day of the week. However, two heavenly figures (two witnesses) announce that Jesus is risen (Lk. 24:1–12). Resurrection was considered the event par excellence of the restoration. The resurrection of Jesus assures the listeners that the restoration begun through Jesus is trustworthy. The meal at Emmaus interprets the sacred meal of the community: When they break the loaf, they experience the presence of the risen Jesus with them (Lk. 24:28–32).

As Luke ends, Jesus commissions the church to announce repentance and forgiveness in Jesus' name to the Gentiles ("to all nations"). Jesus promises to send the Holy Spirit ("power from on high," 24:44–49), though he must first ascend to heaven, the arena from which the Spirit will come.

While Acts does not contain a prologue (as does Luke), Acts 1:1 prompts listeners to remember the prologue to Luke as we begin hearing Acts.

According to Acts 1:6–11 (cf. Acts 2:34; 7:56), Jesus ascends to the right hand of God in heaven. In antiquity, the right hand is the hand of authority. Listeners realize that Jesus' power is greater than any figure on earth, even greater than the Jewish leaders and Roman officials. Although it may be difficult to follow Jesus on the Way, the church can continue because it is under the aegis of the one at the right hand of God.

Jesus prescribes the organizational pattern of Acts: "You will be my witnesses in Jerusalem, in all Judea and Samaria, and to the ends of the earth" (Acts 1:8). The story in Acts then traces the Christian witness as it moves from Jerusalem and Judea (Acts 1:1–8:3) to Samaria (8:4–25) and the ends of the earth (9:1–28:31). The witness to the ends of the earth is itself divided into three parts: in the eastern Mediterranean (9:1–15:35), in the middle Mediterranean (15:36–21:16), and on the way to (and in) Rome (21:17–28:31).

The Witness of the Church to the Realm of God in Jerusalem and Judea: Acts 2:1—8:3

This section of the narrative describes the witness of the early Christian community to the realm of God in Jerusalem and Judea. The continuity of this witness with Judaism is underscored when the first event takes place at Pentecost (Acts 2:1–41). Pentecost was a traditional Jewish festival that celebrated a successful harvest. Luke uses this festival as a symbol of the eschatological ingathering: As people gather the harvest of the field, so God is beginning the ingathering of the harvest of world history. The Holy Spirit empowers the early community in the same way that it fell on Jesus at his baptism (Lk. 3:21–22). At Babel, God confused the human community through different languages (Gen. 11:1–9). The Spirit restores the capacity to understand one another.

Peter preaches on Joel 2:28–32. However, Peter amends the opening words of the text to include "in the last days." This addition places Pentecost, the succeeding narrative, and the church in Luke's day in the last days of the current generation of history (Acts 2:22–36). As God moves toward restoring the world, the curse of Genesis 3:9–16 is somewhat ameliorated. God restores people to their places in the social world that God originally intended; women join men as prophets and leaders in the community. Repentance, baptism, and receiving the Holy Spirit become the means by which people indicate their readiness to join God in the movement toward restoration (Acts 2:38). Christian Judaism is inherently a communal religion with a common life that includes apostolic instruction, fellowship, prayer, praise, and sharing all things (Acts 2:42–47; cf. 4:32–5:1–11; 6:1–7; 11:27–29).

Luke immediately tells a story that becomes a pattern in the narrative of the church in Acts. The apostles witness to the restoration by healing (3:1–9) and interpreting the miracle through preaching (3:10–26). The healing demonstrates the universal restoration in miniature. The apostolic sermon interprets the meaning of Jesus' ministry, points out the antipathy toward him from Jewish authorities, and signals the listeners that the mission to the Gentiles (a part of the universal restoration) is a means by which God is keeping the divine promises to Abraham and Sarah. In response, some Jewish officials arrest the apostolic witnesses (4:1–22). When questioned, the apostles defend their behavior and further interpret the reign of God as the restoration of all things. Although the Jewish leaders intimidate the apostles, God saves the witnesses just as God led Jesus to safety after the synagogue crowd attempted to kill Jesus (cf. Lk. 4:29–30).

Luke provides Acts 4:32–37 as a positive vision of Christian community that sharply contrasts with the hostile Jewish community in the preceding verses. Yet the story of Ananias and Sapphira does not permit the church to develop an attitude of uncritical Christian superiority. Ananias and Sapphira represent Christians who undercut the movement toward restoration (Acts 5:1–11).

The pattern we saw in Acts 3:1–4:22 occurs again in 5:17–42. Christian witnesses are jailed by Jewish leaders (as Jesus anticipated in Lk. 21:12–19). God uses an angel to unlock the prison doors. This narrative reminds the listener that God will providentially care for the church as for Israel in antiquity. The Lukan author impresses this motif on the listener by telling this story in three settings (Acts 5:17–21; 12:6–11; 16:23–29).

Gamaliel illustrates the fact that Luke does not unilaterally or universally condemn Jewish leaders. Luke honors Gamaliel as a respected leader of the Pharisees. Gamaliel weighs the testimony of the apostles and concludes that the Jewish authorities should not work against the Jesus movement. If they leave that movement alone, time will reveal whether God blesses it (Acts 5:33–39).

Within the church a conflict develops between Hebrew-speaking widows and Greek-speaking Jewish widows (Hellenists). The narratives show that God uses the community to mediate providence for both groups and that the early church adapted its organization to account for new situations (Acts

6:1–7). Through deacons, God brings good news to the widows, who are included in the poor of Luke 4:18.

The life and activity of the early Christian community parallel the life and activity of Jesus. Hence we are not surprised that the death of Stephen is much like the death of Jesus: groundless charges, witnesses who do not agree, Jewish dissidents stirring up the crowd, senseless death. However, Stephen demonstrates trust in God by dying in the manner of Jesus (Acts 6:1–8:1; cf. Lk. 22:47–23:49). Stephen interprets the Jewish behavior in the language of Jewish prophets (Acts 7:51–52; cf. Ex. 32:9; 33:3–5; 34:9; Lev. 26:41; Deut. 9:6, 13; 10:16; 31:27; Jer. 4:4; 6:10; 9:26; 17:23; 19:15). Listeners thus discover that the Jewish leaders betray the best of their tradition.

As this segment ends, we meet Saul (Paul)–the central figure in carrying the news of the reign of God beyond Palestine and into the wider Mediterranean world. Saul supported the stoning of Stephen and persecuted the church (8:1–3). The narrative of Acts encourages us to compare and contrast Saul before and after the revelation that he receives on the road to Damascus.

The Journey through Samaria and toward the Ends of the Earth: Acts 8:4–40

In this short segment the apostolic testimony to the divine dominion moves through Samaria. The Samaritans were kin to the Jewish people, being descended from the Jewish residents who stayed in Palestine at the time the Jewish leaders were exiled in Babylon. The Samaritans evolved a religion that considered only the Pentateuch as sacred scripture. Whereas other Jewish people worshiped on Mount Zion (Jerusalem), the primary Samaritan worship center was Mount Gerizim. Relationships between the Jewish and Samaritan communities were usually tense. This part of Acts reminds us that the reign of God will bring about reunion of Samaritan and Jewish communities (Acts 8:4–25).

The witness of Philip to the eunuch from Ethiopia is another step in the journey of the witness to the realm of God to the ends of the earth (Acts 8:26–40; cf. Acts 2:39). Isaiah anticipated the ingathering of Ethiopians (and other Africans) in the divine commonwealth (e.g., Isa. 45:14). Furthermore, although eunuchs were valued because they could be trusted to serve women in positions of prominence, many ancient cultures considered them damaged goods (to use our contemporary vernacular). Isaiah anticipates the day when they will be restored (Isa. 56:3–4).

Witness to the Reign of God Journeys into the Eastern Mediterranean: Acts 9:1—15:35

From now until the end of Acts, the author of Luke–Acts tells the story of the journey of the witness to the reign of God toward the ends of the earth. The current part of the narrative legitimates the movement of the testimony to the reign of God into the eastern Mediterranean world. After encountering the risen Jesus, Saul carries the news to Attalia (about a fourth of the way from Jerusalem to Rome).

Biblical expositors disagree as to whether Acts 9:1–19 is a call or a conversion. A call story describes a call to a mode of serving the God of Israel. A conversion is a fundamental change of perception that involves leaving one religion and entering another. I prefer the former designation because Acts speaks of this event in language that is similar to language found in the calls of Hebrew prophets (Acts 9:15; Isa. 49:1–6; Jer. 1:4–10). The ministry of Paul is to announce the restoration of the Gentiles (Isa. 42:1–7; 49:1–6; Lk. 2:29–30; 3:4–5; 4:16–30, esp. 25–27; 24:47; Acts 1:8; 2:39). The narrative of Paul's call demonstrates that the legitimation for the Gentile mission comes directly from God. We can see that this idea is immensely important to the Lukan author when we realize that he tells it three times (9:1–16; 22:1–21; 26:2–23).

Biblical interpreters rightly call attention to the fact that the portrait of Paul in the letters (particularly the ones whose authorship is not disputed) and in Acts have a common core but differing nuances. Both Acts and the letters depict Paul as missionary to the Gentiles. However, there are also differences. Based on Acts alone, we would never know that Paul wrote a single letter. The chronology of Paul's missionary journeys is slightly different in the two bodies of literature. According to

Acts, for instance, Paul goes straightaway to Damascus and Jerusalem after the encounter with Jesus on the Damascus road, but Galatians says that he was in Arabia for three years (Gal. 1:17–20). Acts dates the apostolic council to Paul's third visit to Jerusalem, yet Galatians places it during the missionary's second visit (Gal. 2:1–10). The Paul of Acts is a powerful orator in the Greek tradition, while the letter-writing Paul speaks of himself as weak in physical appearance (2 Cor. 10:10). In Acts, Paul works many miracles, yet we would have no idea that Paul performed miracles on the basis of the letters only. In Acts, Paul supports the apostolic decree with its admonition for Gentiles to follow limited behaviors that are characteristic of Judaism (Acts 15:28–29; 21:25). The Paul of the letters never mentions such a letter. The Lukan author does not typically refer to Paul as an apostle. Thus, some interpreters believe that the author intentionally denies that title to Paul because Paul does not fulfill the usual criteria for an apostle in Luke and Acts (Acts 1:21–23; but contrast Acts 14:4). Paul, of course, describes himself by that title (1 Cor. 15:5–8; Gal. 1:11–2:10). The Lukan author's rewriting of his sources is so thorough that many scholars conclude that, while Acts doubtless contains historical reminiscences of Paul, we cannot separate them from the author's revisions.

The author of Luke–Acts also offers theological justification for the Gentile mission by appealing to the experience of Peter (Acts 10:1–48). God implants a vision in the Gentile Cornelius to send for Peter, who is a paradigm of Christian Judaism (vv. 1–8). God implants in Peter the vision of eating unclean foods (vv. 9–16). (Scholars point out that ancient authors sometimes used two visions in tandem to communicate that the events described in the visions are divinely controlled.) Peter says to Cornelius and the listeners to Acts, "God shows no partiality" (v. 34). When the Gentiles receive the Holy Spirit, we know that the Gentile mission is of God (v. 47). While the early Christian witness is highly successful (Acts 11:19–29), it also generates considerable opposition (12:1–25), as we expect from Acts 3–4.

The Lukan author does not send Paul on the first missionary journey until the narrative has shown that *God* authorizes it. On this journey, Jewish audiences first react to the preachers with varying combinations of curiosity, receptivity, and hostility (e.g., Acts 13:4–12; 13:13–47; 13:50–51; 14:1–5; 14:19–20). Gentiles are more positive in their response (e.g., Acts 13:4–12; 13:48–49; 14:1–5; 14:8–18).

The Lukan author has now established that God invites Gentiles into the community that witnesses to the restoration. However, we do not know how persons of Jewish and Gentile origin will relate to one another in light of the customs of Israel. Acts 15:1–29, sometimes called the apostolic council (though that title does not appear in the Second Testament), settles this question. A delegation from the Pauline mission in Antioch visits the church at Jerusalem. Christian Pharisees argue that Gentiles should "keep the law of Moses" (Acts 15:5), that is, they should convert to Judaism. Peter and James, themselves faithful to Judaism, disagree (Acts 15:6–21). Their rationale derives from (a) the revelation that Peter received in Acts 10–11, (b) the experience of the Gentiles receiving the Holy Spirit, (c) the admission that the law is "a yoke that neither our ancestors nor we have been able to bear" (Acts 15:10), (d) the signs and wonders that God worked through Barnabas and Paul, and (e) their interpretation of the testimony of scripture (Acts 15:16–17).

A vigorous discussion eventuates in response to the impetus of the Spirit in the Council drafting the so-called apostolic letter (or decree). "For it has seemed good to the Holy Spirit and to us to impose on you no further burden than these essentials: that you abstain from what has been sacrificed to idols and from blood and from what is strangled and from fornication. If you keep yourselves from these, you will do well" (Acts 15:28–29). These norms are reminiscent of instructions for Gentiles who live as aliens in Israel (Lev. 17:3, 10–14; 18:6–30; cf. Ex. 34:15–16; Lev. 3:17; 19:26; Deut. 12:16, 23–27). They are also reminiscent of the Noachic commandments (based on Gen. 9:3–4), articulated fully by later rabbis as guidance for the entire human family. The Noachic laws make it possible for Gentiles to live righteously.[3] Gentiles must cease idol worship and observe some basic Jewish dietary customs. According to the Lukan author, these norms honor the heart of Judaism.

When Gentiles observe them, Christian Jewish people and Gentile Christians can work together. This letter prescribes modest forms of Judaizing Gentiles and depaganizing them.

Witness to the Divine Rule Journeys to the Middle Mediterranean: Acts15:36—21:16

This phase of the witness to the reign of God demonstrates the continuing power of the Holy Spirit and the wisdom of the apostolic letter as the missionaries journey further west to Beroea and Corinth (roughly two thirds of the distance from Jerusalem to Rome). Silas and Timothy join Paul as central characters. The Spirit calls Paul to preach in Macedonia (Acts 16:6–10). Lydia, a prominent woman in the commercial sector and a God-fearer (a Gentile who is attracted to Judaism but has not converted), is welcomed into the community of the restoration through baptism (Acts 16:11–15).

Recalling earlier themes, Jewish people in Thessalonica become enraged at the Christian witnesses and make a pact with thugs in the area to put Paul on trial. A vigilante group seizes Jason (who is curious about the Way) and claims that the church believes in "another king [besides Caesar] named Jesus" (Acts 17:7). Listeners know that the charge is both untrue and true. The Christian community does not seek to overthrow Caesar through revolution, but the Christian community knows that Caesar's power is temporary. In this atmosphere of narrative ambiguity, Paul arrives in Athens, a potent theological-geographical symbol of the height of Hellenistic philosophy and theology. On the Areopagus, Paul refers to an inscription "to an unknown God" (Acts 17:16–34) almost as if preaching from a text. On the one hand, Paul confirms that the Athenians have some knowledge of God through nature and their own philosophers. However, Paul makes it clear that their knowledge is partial and that, in order to come to a fuller awareness of God, they need to repent and embrace the God of Israel.

While Paul is visiting Corinth, the Lukan author mentions that the missionary is a tentmaker (i.e., someone who made tents and other goods out of leather). Day by day Paul labors alongside Aquila and Priscilla, Jewish believers who were expelled from Rome (with other Jewish persons) by Claudius (Acts 18:1–4). The preaching of Paul and Silas yields a mixed response from the local Jewish community (Acts 18:5–11). When some of the Jewish folk attempt to press charges against Paul, the Roman official Gallio will not hear the case because the proconsul recognizes it is not a serious crime (Acts 18:12–17). In this instance, as in several others, Rome saves Christians from Jewish attack. By recounting how Paul had taken a Nazarite vow (a promise to dedicate oneself to God and to serve God by going beyond the usual requirements of Judaism) and then cut his hair, Acts reinforces that Paul continued to live as a faithful participant in Judaism (Acts 18:18–23; Num. 6:1–21; cf. Acts 21:20–26). Apollos, a famous Jewish leader from Alexandria, symbolizes the need for solid instruction in the church (Acts 18:24–28). The Lukan author underscores the importance of fullness of initiation into the community of the restoration by having Paul lay hands on persons who have received only the baptism of John. Through Paul these disciples now receive the Holy Spirit (Acts 19:1–7).

God works miracles through Paul (19:11–19). The Ephesian silversmiths become frustrated and initiate a riot when the witness to the reign of God deprives them of income. A local official silences the crowd, protecting Paul and his companions (Acts 19:23–41). Listeners realize that the Ephesian silversmiths need not be anxious about economic security. Through the church, God provides materially. The silversmiths could share in this providence by turning from their idols (Acts 2:42–47; 4:32–5:11; 6:1–7; cf. 11:27–29).

Paul resolves to visit Jerusalem for the last time (Acts 20:1–12; cf. Lk. 8:40–56). During Paul's instruction to the elders of the church in Ephesus, Luke reveals the essential work of the elders of the later Lukan church: to ground the community in the knowledge that the realm of God is being manifested afresh. This teaching can protect the community from deceivers from without and wolves from within (Acts 20:17–36). Paul gets to Jerusalem under divine providence, mediated by the Spirit (Acts 21:1–6). In Jerusalem, a Christian prophet prepares us to realize that Paul will meet a fate similar to that of Jesus (Acts 21:7–16).

Witness to the Restoration Journeys to Rome through Paul's Imprisonment: Acts 21:17—28:31

When Paul arrives in Jerusalem, he immediately discovers a false rumor that he has been advocating that Jewish people forsake the law (Acts 21:17–36; see also 16:3; 18:18; 20:16). When yet another vigilante group seeks to murder the missionary, Caesar's soldiers save him (Acts 21:17–36).

An agent of Caesar, a tribune, makes it possible for Paul to witness to the reign of God by means of a defense in which the traveler tells the story of his encounter with the risen Jesus on the road to Damascus (Acts 21:37–22:21; 9:1–19). When the crowd becomes boisterous, the Romans join the Jewish community of Luke 23 in violation of their own legal customs. The Romans flog Paul in order "to find out the reason for this outcry." Paul himself calls them to task. "Is it legal for you to flog a Roman citizen who is uncondemned?" (Acts 22:22–29). While we have known since Acts 16:1 that Paul is a Roman citizen, we realize anew the universal power of God, for God uses even this citizenship to transport the witness to the divine rule to Rome. Only a handful of persons living in the Mediterranean world became citizens. Roman citizenship afforded one rights and protections not available to others. Mistreatment of a citizen was a crime.

The narrative is now electric with tension. As soon as the Roman official turns the missionary over to a Jewish council "the dissension became violent." The Roman official saves Paul from harm (Acts 22:30–23:35).

When the governor, Felix, attempts to pursue charges (with the help of a high priest and an attorney, Acts 24:1–9), Paul depicts himself as a model of Jewish faithfulness (Acts 24:10–23). While Roman officials often act as agents of protection for Paul, Felix demonstrates immediately why Rome is not ultimately trustworthy. The governor wants a bribe and allows the missionary to languish in prison for two years (Acts 24:24–27). The replacement governor, Festus, gives attention to Paul's case, thus giving the Lukan author the opportunity to give the narrative a decisive turn. Paul draws on his right as a citizen to bring his situation to the supreme tribunal in Rome (Acts 25:1–12).

Festus welcomes the sovereign Herod Agrippa II and his sister Bernice. They listen to Paul intently and think him innocent (Acts 25:13–26:1). Their visit gives the Lukan author the occasion to recount Paul's encounter with the risen Jesus a third time (Acts 26:2–32).

Paul takes advantage of the seafaring opportunities afforded people in the Hellenistic age by sailing to Rome. Alas, the trip takes place when the seasons are changing. Paul predicts a storm (typical of such times). When Paul's prediction proves accurate, the listeners' confidence is increased in Paul as preacher and Luke as narrator (Acts 27:1–12): What they say is reliable. The people on the ship believe they will drown (Acts 27:13–20). However, divine guidance again appears in the form of an angel who confirms that Paul will survive in order to preach before the emperor (Acts 27:21–44). We are reminded once more that the providence of the God of Israel will carry the church through the storms of witnessing to the divine rule.

On the island of Malta, Luke stresses Paul's innocence. A snake bites the missionary, but Paul shakes it off like a dry leaf. The Lukan author reminds us that the Holy Spirit is powerfully with Paul by telling how the missionary was the agent through whom God healed a sick person (Acts 28:1–10).

Rome is a preeminent symbol of the Gentile world. The listener knows that while Rome is somewhat ambiguous in Luke–Acts, it will ultimately be judged for its idolatry, falsehood, and violence. Yet God has brought Paul to Rome to preach the news of the universal restoration and to offer Rome the opportunity to repent and be renewed.

Paul, following a missionary pattern in Acts, goes first to the Jewish community. When some people dispute Paul's announcement that the divine rule is being manifest afresh, Paul turns to Isaiah 6:9–10 to say that God is now hardening Israel's heart (even as God hardened Pharaoh's heart) so that they will not repent (Acts 28:26–27). Instead, the "salvation of God has been sent to the Gentiles; they will listen" (Acts 28:17–31).

Christians today sometimes think that the ending of Acts is odd. The book ends with Paul's preaching and teaching in Rome (Acts 28:30–31). What happens to Paul? Although the narrative does not specify the fate of the missionary traveler, we have known since Luke 9 that the followers of Jesus are to take up their crosses. In Acts 21, the author explicitly stated that Paul's witness would end as Jesus' did. This way of concluding Luke–Acts puts a question before the listeners. Will we witness to the divine restoration of the world, now manifest afresh through Jesus, as boldly in our world as Paul did in his? Do we have sufficient trust in God to face the difficulties, and even suffering, that sometimes follow from such witness?

Today's Church Is Commissioned to Witness to the Divine Rule

The risen Jesus commissions the church to witness to the divine rule (Lk. 24:44–53; Acts 1:6–11) in the midst of a world of brokenness, idolatry, social segregation, poverty, sickness, enmity with nature, and death. This commission still pertains to the church in twenty-first-century North America.

The hermeneutic of analogy (discussed earlier in chapter 2) can help the congregation name ways in which today's world is similar to the world of Luke–Acts. Some of the broken conditions take different forms today than they did in the world of the first century, but the essential experience is much the same. For example, few contemporary households have statues of idols on the mantel in the family room, but many of us functionally regard finite objects, activities, or values as ultimate. Our world is marked by poverty, exploitation, various kinds of social segregation, destructive relationships with nature, violence, and death.

The fundamental calling of the preacher is to help the congregation recognize that God is always present and always seeking to restore this world so that all relationships and situations manifest the divine presence. The preacher is called to help the congregation understand the content of the divine realm and to help the congregation identify relationships and circumstances through which the divine rule is coming to expression. The preacher can encourage the congregation to welcome contemporary agents through whom this manifestation is coming about. The sermon can especially lead the congregation to recognize how, through the Holy Spirit, they can become a community of the divine realm, whose interior relationships model God's purposes and modes of relationship, and whose exterior relationships call attention to God's purposes of restoration in all things.

A caution: Most preachers easily find vivid, deeply moving analogies between the brokenness of the ancient world and the brokenness of the world today. Preachers typically have a much more difficult time identifying positive situations in today's world that demonstrate the presence and hope of the divine rule. While the community needs to understand and feel the broken aspects of the world, it is imperative for the sermon to contain discussion and description of the reign of God that are at least as powerful and penetrating. When such positive material is not in the sermon, the congregation may subtly get the impression that the reign of brokenness is more powerful than that of God. The community can lose confidence in the divine aegis and, in consequence, lose energy for witness. Positive commentary and examples bolster the community's confidence that God is actually present and can help motivate them for bold witness. When the preacher describes specific embodiments of the divine reign, the congregation can use these sermonic examples as lenses through which to recognize its occurrence in their everyday life and seek to join it.

The apocalyptic timetable of the reign of God in Luke–Acts raises theological issues for the preacher. Although the Lukan author prepared the early Christian community for a delay in the arrival of the apocalypse, he hardly envisioned a postponement of two millennia. The preacher needs to help the congregation deal with this phenomenon.

Some Christians respond that God's notion of time differs from ours. "With the Lord one day is like a thousand years" (2 Pet. 3:8; Ps. 90:4). The delay that seems prolonged to us is but a short time for God. While this reply may seem intelligible to some people, it is unintelligible to others. Since the resurrection and ascension, the number of people who suffer multiplies every year. According to basic logic, a God of unconditional love and unrelenting will for justice would not subject the world to a tribulation of two thousand years and more.

It makes more sense to regard aspects of the apocalyptic dimension of the reign of God as elements of a first-century worldview that can help us by way of analogy, even if we cannot embrace every specific element of apocalypticism. The abiding value of the apocalyptic vision is to remind the community that the present condition of the world is not the way God intends and that God continues to work to restore the world. The apocalypse may not occur as a singular event, but the literary figure of the apocalypse bespeaks God's intention not to give up on the world; God perpetually works with the world in order to help it manifest God's aims of love and justice.

The preacher needs also to address the issue of divine power. Apocalypticism assumes that God can act unilaterally to intervene in the world in a single, transforming moment.[4] I join many other Christians today in thinking that though God is more powerful than any other force, God cannot act in that way. A major difference between divine power and all other kinds of power is that divine power is inexhaustible. It never runs out. It never stops seeking the good. God is present in every situation, doing all that God can do to help each circumstance manifest as much as it can of the reign of God.

Luke–Acts, together with the story of Israel, provides a clue to ways in which God is at work in the world today. As I noted above, for the early Christian community, Jesus interprets the cross and resurrection as demonstrating the nature of divine power (9:18–27). God's power is ironically expressed through self-giving love that is willing to suffer for the renewal of community. This pattern was already present in Israel. This pattern reconceives the nature and exercise of power as a key in the restoration of the community.

Israel, Jesus, and the early church appeared to be insignificant forces in the world: a tiny nation on a side street of the ancient Near East; an itinerant carpenter who was murdered; a small group of people who claimed that a Jewish person crucified on the side street had been raised from the dead as a decisive sign that the transformation of the cosmos was underway. What could be less impressive? However, God worked through them to manifest restoration. The preacher can help the congregation identify situations today that are similar–situations that appear to be less than they are in their ability to help restore the world. Indeed, the divine rule is often ironic in its appearance.

A Sermon on the Theme of the Reign of God

After something bad happens, you often hear people make comments that indicate that such occurrences are normal. Someone says, "That's just the way things are." And you hear a sigh of resignation.

Thanksgiving dinner with the in-laws and grandparents present: that's when your children start a food fight, launching olives like atom bombs. As you turn red from embarrassment and frustration, Grandma pats you on the arm. "The way the world is these days, what can you expect from kids?"

In a run-down part of town, the storm drains and the sewers are connected. During a heavy rain, the pipes overload so that the sewers back into the basements of the houses at the same time that they spew untreated waste into the nearby river. When asked to fix the problem, the city council doesn't have the money. Of course, the council finds mega-bucks for airport improvement. "What can you expect in this world?"

A fifty-year-old drops dead from a heart attack. "A tragedy. But," we say with a shrug of the shoulders, "those things happen." A world collapses, and the most sensitive comment that some can offer is, "Those things happen."

A lot of people live under a cloud of resignation. "The circumstances of this world are just the way things are." And the implication is, "We can't hope for anything better." So you learn how to make your way among the pieces of brokenness. Some people even learn how to profit from the brokenness. They want the rest of us to think that brokenness is normal.

Many people felt much that way at the time of Luke. The Roman army occupied the whole Mediterranean world, maintaining the *Pax Romana*, the peace of Rome, a social quiet that resulted from fear of the Roman sword. Taxation hung around the necks of people like hundred-pound weights. Many people sold themselves into slavery to pay their bills, while the wealthy grew wealthier as a result of this exploitation. Rancor was the standard relationship between many ethnic groups. Periodic famines created wheat shortages that led to bread riots. Not many years before, a volcano had buried Pompeii. In the ash you can still see the imprint of people trying to escape but who were buried alive. The Gentiles turned to their idols, but their idols were silent.

In that world, in an out-of-the-way synagogue in the out-of-the-way town of Nazareth, Jesus was the guest preacher. Jesus read from the prophet Isaiah, "The Spirit of the Lord is upon me, because [God] has anointed me to bring good news to the poor...to proclaim release to the captives and recovery of sight to the blind...to proclaim the year of the Lord's favor" (Lk. 4:18–19). Like a preacher slowly closing the Bible after the reading of scripture and slipping it under the pulpit, Jesus rolls up the scroll and says, "Today this scripture has been fulfilled in your hearing" (4:21).

The congregation knew what Jesus meant. The Jewish people of the time associated that passage with the realm of God–the time when everything in the world would be the way that God wants it to be. All relationships. All circumstances. God would restore the world to its original purposes so that it would again be like the garden of Eden.

Your children: models of creativity, clear and pleasant communication, and worthwhile contributions to the world. Poverty replaced by abundance for all. Exploitation gives way to support. Groups that used to fuss and fight now work together. People are joined in real *community.* Nature, too, is renewed. Every wind is gentle. Every rain is just enough. Every field is burgeoning with produce. No more trips to the hospital. You've made your last visit to the funeral home.

"Today this scripture has been fulfilled." According to the gospel of Luke, the process of transformation from the old age to the realm of God is now underway through Jesus Christ. According to Acts, the church witnesses to this transformation.

- Jesus teaches, "Love your enemies; do good to those who hate you," and we realize that the reign of God creates a new social world in which all people support one another.
- Jesus eats with tax collectors and sinners, and we realize that God remakes all relationships.
- Jesus heals a bent-over woman, and we realize that God wills to restore all.

- Jesus feeds five thousand in the wilderness, and we realize that God wills to feed all.

- Jesus calms a storm-tossed sea, and we realize that God intends for nature to be an instrument of blessing.

- God raises Jesus from the dead, and we realize that not even the power of death can stand in the way of the new age.

- The Holy Spirit falls on the church at Pentecost, and we realize that the Spirit empowers the church to continue the ministry of Jesus.

- Peter heals a beggar who lies lame at the temple gate.

- People share their goods and wealth as in Eden, so that they have no poor.

- In a great reunion of the human race, Jewish and Gentile folk embrace.

- When apostles are imprisoned, God opens the prison doors.

- Roman officials protect Paul from violent mobs and become the means by which Paul carries the gospel to Rome.

- Yes, through the disciples in Acts, God even raises the dead.

First-century people know what these things mean. God is restoring the world.

However, along the way Jesus and the church encounter opposition. Some traditional authorities oppose Jesus and maneuver to have the Romans put him to death. Similar authorities harass many of the early Christian witnesses, trumping up false charges that send Paul to Rome, even stoning Stephen.

These stories are sobering. However, Luke includes them for a purpose. No matter how good the news of the reign of God, some people and systems oppose it. Some of them do not believe it. Some misunderstand it and think that they have too much to lose if it comes. If I made my living selling guns, for instance, I would not want a world premised on loving enemies. Who would buy guns in such a world? I would resist such a world. Luke's tales of opposition are a pastoral word to remind *us* that *we* can expect opposition when we witness to the reign of God.

However, do you notice something strange about the way in which the realm of God is underway through Jesus and the church? Jesus and the church appear to be less than they are. Although Bible readers sometimes get the impression that Palestine was the center of the ancient world, it was actually a tiny nation on a side street of the Mediterranean. Jesus was from a county seat town in a relatively poor rural area. Without impressive formal credentials, he worked a few miracles, taught a handful of disciples, and was crucified. The earliest Christian community was much the same—people who did not have many formal credentials and who claimed that a Jewish person crucified on their side street had been raised from the dead as a sign that the transformation of the cosmos was underway.

What could be less impressive? Yet the crucifixion of a Jewish person on the edge of the empire becomes an occasion for God to demonstrate the renewal of the world. This turn of events helps us realize that God works through similar people and circumstances today to witness to the fact that the divine power that wills to restore the world is still at work among us.

The divine reign sometimes comes to expression through the Christian community. For example, about seventy years ago, the church building of the congregation of which I am a part, University Park Christian Church (Disciples of Christ), was located in another neighborhood in Indianapolis. However, the congregation decided to move, according to a quote from the official church history, because of the "encroachment of colored peoples."

After the congregation relocated, it called Gerald L. K. Smith as pastor during the late 1920s and early 1930s. Smith was one of the most prominent racists and anti-Semites in the history of the Christian Church (Disciples of Christ). He published a national newsletter that promulgated hate for African American and Jewish peoples. After he moved to Louisiana, he was publicly associated with the Ku Klux Klan and Governor Huey Long. During his pastorate in Indianapolis, thousands of people joined our congregation. Indeed, during one summer revival more than seven hundred people came forward in one week.

Yet in the intervening years, the Spirit of the reign of God has worked through other pastors and elders and Bible school teachers who did not share Smith's views. Today, University Park is a predominately European American congregation that jointly owns its building with Faith United Christian Church, a predominately African American congregation. The two communities worship together several times a year and work with one another in several important ministries.

Now, to be honest, this situation is not a complete manifestation of the divine rule. Some people left both University Park and Faith United when the two communities covenanted together. At one level, it is embarrassing for two congregations of the same denomination to continue to exist in the same building as two congregations.(I like to think that the Holy Spirit prompts this uneasiness as a way of nudging the two congregations toward greater union.) But two generations ago, who could have imagined the change that has taken place in University Park, and the willingness of Faith United to risk sharing its life with a church with the rancid past of University Park? The rule of God is not fully manifest, but the changes that have taken place at the corner of 46th and Illinois (the location of the church building) suggest that further transformation may be ahead.

In any event, the divine rule is much larger than the life of the church. Sometimes, in fact, the church gets in the way of the divine reign. When the church becomes an obstacle, God moves outside the Christian community for restoration.

After I had watched *Schindler's List* several times, it finally dawned on me to think of Oskar Schindler's situation along these lines. Most of the leaders of Nazi Germany who engineered the Holocaust were baptized Christians. While several German Churches protested these developments through the Barmen Declaration, other Christian leaders blessed Nazism and even provided theological justification for anti-Semitism.

Oskar Schindler drank too much, womanized, lied too easily, and too often manipulated circumstances for his own benefit. But when push came to shove, God used these very qualities as instruments through which to save the lives of the Jewish workers in his factories. Schindler may not have prevented the Holocaust, but he became an unlikely witness to God's desire that life prevail, even when leaders of the church offered an invocation over the mentality of death.

What are we supposed to do when we encounter this restoring power? Luke is very clear. We repent of our complicity with those people and powers that oppose the divine reign. We participate with God and communities that seek to embody the divine rule. Most of us church people are more relaxed when we can deal with other church people than when we have to work with the Oskar Schindlers of the world. But we are called to work with whoever is available, just as the people in the congregation at Jerusalem learned to work with Paul.

A restoration is underway. I pray for the eyes to see it and the heart to be a part of it. I hope you will too.

CHAPTER 4

Preaching on the Holy Spirit

Scholars universally call attention to the central role of the Holy Spirit in Luke–Acts. The Spirit is active in Judaism prior to the birth of Jesus at Bethlehem. The Spirit helps bring Jesus into the world. The public ministry of Jesus takes place under the impetus of the Holy Spirit. The Spirit empowers the church for witness in Acts. This prominence raises questions that are important for the contemporary preacher.

- What is the Holy Spirit for the author of Luke–Acts?
- How is the understanding of the Spirit in Luke–Acts related to the nature and work of the Spirit in the First Testament and in Judaism?
- What does the Spirit do in Luke–Acts? In particular, what is its relationship to Jesus and the reign of God?
- Does the Holy Spirit work similarly in the contemporary setting?

In this chapter, I first summarize understandings of the Holy Spirit in the First Testament and in Judaism in the Hellenistic period (ca. 300 B.C.E. to 200 C.E.) that are important to Luke–Acts. The Lukan author, primarily indebted to notions of Spirit in Judaism, is sympathetic with experiences of the Spirit in the wider Hellenistic setting. The chapter traces the development of the theme of the Spirit in Luke–Acts. A comment on the continuing relevance of the Lukan author's presentation precedes a thematic sermon.

The Holy Spirit in Judaism

In the First Testament and the literature of Judaism in the Hellenistic era, the Spirit is a noncorporeal representative through whom God works in the world. The Spirit is an instrument through which divine power operates.

The character of the Holy Spirit is revealed in the etymology of the word "spirit" in both Hebrew and Greek. Both the Hebrew term *ruach* and the Greek *pneuma* can be rendered "wind" or "breath" as well as "spirit." The nature and movement of wind or breath is analogous to that of the Spirit. We cannot see wind; it can move without hindrance. It has power; it causes things to happen. The experience of the Spirit is much like the experience of the wind. Breath, too, can move freely. It has power and causes things to happen. Breath animates persons and animals.

Likewise, although we cannot see the Spirit, it is present. It has power. It is not confined. It moves across the vast spaces of the cosmos like the wind moving across the open fields. The Holy Spirit causes things to happen. On the analogy of breath, writers in the Bible occasionally speak of its filling a person or a community. It animates. The Spirit is to the world as breath to the body.

At the risk of oversimplification, we can say that the Spirit operates in Judaism in five ways.[1] Though I speak of these modes separately, they interrelate.[2]

First, the Spirit is a divine tool in creation and re-creation. The Holy Spirit is present at the creation of the world (Gen. 1:1–2). All life derives from the breath of God (e.g., Gen. 2:7). God sends forth the Spirit to create new entities (e.g., Ps. 104:30). When the community is the same as dead, God re-creates it through the Spirit (e.g., Isa. 32:15–20; Ezek. 36:26–27).

Second, the Spirit is universally present sustaining the world (e.g., Ps. 139:7–12; Wis. 1:7). Indeed, the Spirit even preserved the primeval chaotic sea before God began to create (Gen. 1:2). When God withdraws the Spirit, life ceases (e.g., Job 34:14). Through the Spirit God helps the community (e.g., Ps. 143:10).

Third, the Holy Spirit fills or anoints people. Often, the Spirit moves people to ecstasy (e.g., Num. 11:24–25). People have an intense awareness of the presence of the Spirit, sometimes overflowing in dramatic manifestations, for example, speaking in tongues.

Fourth, and closely related, this infilling is typically for the purpose of empowering persons for specific tasks. Under the influence of the Spirit, Gideon, for instance, leads the community successfully (e.g., Judg. 6:33–35). The First Testament highlights the role of the Spirit in bringing God's word to expression. The Spirit fills many of the prophets to prepare them to speak God's oracles of judgment and salvation in the community (e.g., Ezek. 1:1–4; Isa. 6:1–6; 48:16; 61:1–11).

Fifth, for communities in the stream leading to apocalypticism, the manifestation of the Spirit is a sign that the world is moving toward eschatological consummation (e.g., Isa. 34:16; 44:1–5; Joel 2:28–29; Zech. 12:10–13; 2 Macc. 7:23; 14:46; *Testament of Judah* 24:3). These communities regard the Spirit as "guarantee," "downpayment," or "first fruit" of the new age. The Spirit helps repair the fallen world.

Many other religious communities in antiquity had similar understandings of religious ecstasy and spirit. An eminent historian of Greek religion, E. R. Dodds, points out that intense religious feeling (similar to category three above) is a component of many Greek religions. Devotees enter a state of ecstasy. The purpose of such states is to communicate to human beings the sense that they have access to the incredible energy of the deity. People emerge from such experiences filled with new confidence for life. Some Greek religions taught that through ecstasy human beings achieved a measure of union with the god who was the focus of worship.[3]

Jewish traditions thus share some understanding of phenomena of the Spirit with other religions of Luke's time (e.g., emphasis on ecstasy as a validating religious experience) even while maintaining critical differences (e.g., the Jewish community never believed that human beings could achieve union with deity).

The Holy Spirit in Luke–Acts

Luke presumes understandings of the Holy Spirit that were prevalent in the First Testament and in Judaism. The events of Luke–Acts lead listeners to recognize that events in the narrative are under the guidance of the God of Israel through the instrumentality of the Holy Spirit. The five themes discussed above all recur in the Lukan author's two volumes.

The Narrative Prepares the Listener to Recognize the Spirit (Lk. 1:5—2:52)

When Zechariah is at prayer, an angel confirms that John will be filled with the Spirit (Lk. 1:15). Elizabeth and Zechariah are filled with the Spirit and interpret the ministry of Jesus as a signal that the realm of God is being manifested (1:41, 67). Other people are later filled with the Spirit.

Similarly, the Spirit rests on Simeon, revealing that the aged prophet will see the agent of the reign of God before dying. The Spirit guides Simeon to the temple to see the child (Lk. 2:25–27). This incident prepares hearers to recognize that the Spirit sometimes leads the community through visions.

The Holy Spirit is responsible for the birth of Jesus (Lk. 1:35). When Jesus announces the re-creation of the world and engages in activities that embody the great restoration, the listener hears an echo of the story of the role of the Spirit at the creation and takes heart: As God created once, so God is moving to create again.

These first references to being filled and led by the Spirit are a guide for understanding later occurrences. People who are filled with the Spirit carry out ministries similar to those of John, Elizabeth, Zechariah, Simeon, and, most of all, Jesus. Commentators frequently point out that these references indicate that the Lukan author sees a prophetic dimension in Luke–Acts. The church, heir to these materials, is subsequently understood as a spirit-filled prophetic community.

The Ministry of Jesus Is the Paradigm of the Spirit-Filled Life (Luke 3:1—Acts 1:26)

These sections of Luke–Acts intimate that the ministry of Jesus and the church occurs under the auspices of the Holy Spirit. John the Baptist indicates that Jesus' purpose is to baptize the world with the Holy Spirit and fire (Lk. 3:17). To be baptized with the Spirit is to be filled with the power that is manifesting the realm of God. The fire refers to judgment.

The baptism of Jesus confirms that Jesus is filled with the Spirit in his public ministry (Lk. 3:21–22). The spirit-filled life of Jesus is thus the pattern for the spirit-filled life of the church in Acts. Because Jesus sends the Spirit on the church (Acts 1:6–8), the church can carry out the same kinds of ministries in Acts and beyond.

The Holy Spirit leads Jesus to be tempted by the devil (Lk. 4:1–13). In this context, temptation refers to the struggle between God and the devil in the last days. This passage, too, is paradigmatic; the church can expect the same kind of eschatological struggle that Jesus faces in the wilderness. The Holy Spirit initiates such confrontations as part of manifesting the reign of God. Furthermore, the text assures the reader that the Holy Spirit sustains the community in the face of such painful struggle. When believers are brought to trial, the Holy Spirit will teach them what to say.[4]

I have previously commented on the ministry of Jesus as revealed in the paradigmatic incident in the synagogue at Nazareth (Lk. 4:16–30). This passage (especially 4:18a, "The Spirit of the Lord is upon me…") reinforces the idea that the whole of Jesus' ministry takes place under the auspices of the Holy Spirit.

The connection between the Spirit and the divine rule is recalled in Luke 11:1–13. After teaching the disciples to pray for the reign of God (11:2–4), Jesus uses a traditional rabbinical mode of argument from the lesser to the greater. If a householder will get up in the middle of the night to provide bread for a needy neighbor, how much more will God manifest the divine rule, which includes the movement of the Holy Spirit (Lk. 11:5–13)?

The Holy Spirit spoke through the instructions of the resurrected Jesus to the disciples. They are to understand Jesus, their life, and the reign of God from the perspective of Moses, the prophets, and the writings (i.e., the First Testament). They are to know that the cross and resurrection reveal how the divine realm operates in the world. They are to preach repentance and forgiveness to Gentiles (Lk. 24:44–49). God will give them power from on high (i.e., the Spirit) for this mission (Acts 1:5, 8).

The Spirit Empowers the Early Christians (Acts 2:1—8:40)

As promised, the Holy Spirit fills and empowers the church as eschatological community. At Pentecost the members of the church received the Spirit together, thus reminding us that the experience and work of the Spirit creates eschatological community (Acts 2:1–4). Pentecost was a harvest festival in Judaism. The outpouring of the Spirit is part of the eschatological harvest that is now underway. The Spirit inspires ecstasy in the community. The description of the Spirit as the rush of a mighty wind recollects the movement of the Spirit at creation and points to the re-creation of the cosmos. The tongues of fire recall the divine presence (e.g., *1 Enoch* 14:8–25), the pillar of fire in the wilderness wandering (Ex. 13:21–22; 14:24), and the making of the covenant at Sinai (Ex. 19:18). God, who was present with Israel as fire at Sinai and as a pillar of fire as Israel journeyed through wilderness to the promised land, is with the church as history moves toward the consummation of the reign of God.

At Babel a united human family spoke one language and sought to usurp God's place. In judgment God scattered the human family and gave each group its own language so that they could not talk with one another (Gen. 11:1–9). The Holy Spirit reverses the confusion wrought at Babel when the people begin to speak and understand languages other than their own (Acts 2:4–13). Whenever bits and pieces of the human family are reunited, their reunion points to the final regeneration.

The Lukan author interprets this movement of the Spirit eschatologically by adding the phrase "in the last days" to the text of Joel 2:28 in Peter's sermon on Pentecost (Acts 2:17). The Spirit will eventually pour out on "all flesh," that is, on Gentiles as well as on the Jewish community. The Spirit will restore relationships between women and men. Females and males prophesy, that is, serve as leaders in the community; old and young see visions for the same purpose. Distinctions between slave and free disappear, as both are prophets, thus anticipating the day when slavery will end (Acts 2:17–18). However, the restoration will not be complete until the apocalypse renews the entire cosmos (Acts 2:19–21).

In the meantime, the preaching of Peter calls listeners to repent of their complicity with the old world, to be baptized into the community of the new age, and to receive the gift of the Spirit (Acts 2:38).

The Spirit creates the church as a community of worship, study, prayer, and sharing all things in common (Acts 2:42–47). The life of the church, at its best, is a foretaste of life in the eschatological world.

Christian preachers sometimes say that the Spirit was silent in Judaism after the close of the First Testament until it reappeared at Pentecost. Although a handful of Jewish texts from antiquity can be cited in this vein, this statement does not represent the general view of Judaism in this period. According to their own testimony, many Jewish people experienced the Spirit at that time (e.g., Wis. 1:7; 9:17; 12:2; Sir. 39:6; *Testament of Levi* 2:3; *1 Enoch* 91:1; *4 Ezra* 5:22; *1QH* 4:31). If we may speak of an unusual dimension of the Spirit from Christian perspective, it is to regard the time of Luke as the last days when the Spirit would help restore the relationship between Jewish and Gentile communities.

Through the power of the Holy Spirit the church witnesses to the rule of God after the pattern of Jesus in the gospel. After Peter and John follow the ministry of Jesus by healing, the Holy Spirit empowers them to preach prophetically. Indeed, just as Jesus promised, the Spirit gives these apostles testimony when they are tried by local authorities (Lk. 12:20; Acts 4:8).

The Spirit is the source of the teaching of the ancestors (Acts 4:25). The listener remembers that Jesus also taught when full of the Spirit. The community, then, knows to respect the teaching of the apostles and other leaders in the community (e.g., Acts 6:3, 5, 10; cf. 11:24, 28; 20:28).

The Holy Spirit fills the early community with ecstasy (e.g., Acts 4:31; cf. 13:52; 19:2–6). As in Israel, ecstasy is not an end in itself but is for the purpose of strengthening the community for witness by imparting a visceral awareness of the presence of the Spirit. Ecstatic occurrences are typically followed by bold acts of witness.

Ananias and Sapphira "put the Spirit…to the test" when they withhold funds from the common treasury (Acts 5:9; cf. v. 3). The Greek word translated "test" (*peiradzo*) is rendered "tempt" in many English translations of Luke 4:1–13. Ananias and Sapphira are in league with Satan in resisting the manifestation of the new world. Luke implies that the Spirit strikes the couple dead. This story echoes in the listener's ear when hearing that some Samaritans want to purchase the power of the Holy Spirit. Peter says to them, "Repent therefore of this wickedness of yours, and pray to the Lord that, if possible, the intent of your heart may be forgiven you" (Acts 8:22).

Stephen's ministry proceeds under the leading of the Spirit along the model of Jesus (Acts 6:10), but conventional authorities stir up the crowd and bring false witnesses against Stephen, just as they did against Jesus (6:10–15). When they accuse Stephen of blasphemy (6:11), Stephen counters that they have forsaken the leading of the Holy Spirit (7:51). The listener concludes that Stephen's opponents have committed blasphemy against the Holy Spirit (cf. Lk. 12:10). The Lukan author pointedly says that at the moment of death, Stephen was "filled with the Holy Spirit." The Spirit gave Stephen a vision of the glory of God (Acts 7:55). Stephen dies as Jesus did, by yielding his spirit (7:59–60). Just as the Spirit was trustworthy to Jesus and Stephen, so the Spirit is trustworthy when later generations encounter opposition to their witness.

As this segment of the narrative draws to a close, an essential characteristic of the Holy Spirit in Luke–Acts comes to expression. The Spirit constantly pushes the Christian community to enlarge its vision of the reign of God and of the community that witnesses to that reign. The Holy Spirit leads Philip to the chariot of the Ethiopian eunuch, where Philip interprets the significance of the manifestation of the reign of God for the eunuch (Acts 8:29). The Spirit is reuniting Samaritans and Ethiopian eunuchs (and others whom they represent) with the God of Israel. The church is to welcome them.

The Spirit Guides the Gentile Mission (Acts 9:1—28:31)

The Holy Spirit now guides the church in following the command of Jesus to witness to the inclusion of Gentiles in the reign of God. After Paul is called to this ministry, he is filled with the Spirit and is thereby empowered in the manner of Jesus, the apostles, and the earlier Christian communities (Acts 9:17).

Similarly, the Spirit brings Peter and Cornelius into relationship and brings Peter before an assembly at Caesarea that includes Gentiles (Acts 10:19; 11:12). In a reprise of Pentecost, the Spirit falls on the Gentiles. The Gentiles are gathered into the community that witnesses to the restoration (Acts 10:44–48; 11:15–16). These stories–the calls of Paul and of Peter, Cornelius, and the Gentiles at Caesarea–impress upon the listener that the Spirit authenticates the Gentile mission.

As the hearers expect, conflict breaks out in the church regarding the validity of the Gentile mission. When the apostolic council convenes in Jerusalem to resolve this issue, the fact that the Gentiles have received the Spirit is one of the essential pieces of evidence (Acts 15:8). This passage offers a valuable insight into the Lukan author's understanding of one way in which the Spirit works in the community. The council listened to the revelation that Peter had received in Acts 10–11, the experience of the Gentiles receiving the Holy Spirit, traditions concerning the law, the signs and wonders that God worked through Barnabas and Paul, and scripture. After listening and conversing, it "seemed good to the Holy Spirit and to us" to welcome the Gentiles into the Christian community on the conditions of Acts 15:29. The Spirit moved through the process of conversation.[5]

The book of Acts contains fewer than a dozen direct references to the Holy Spirit after Acts 15. However, the author has shaped the preceding narrative in such a way that the hearer knows that the story proceeds under the guidance of the Spirit.[6] The implication is that the Spirit continues to empower the church to witness to the reign of God (especially welcome of Gentiles) after the conclusion to Luke–Acts.

The Spirit in the Church and the World Today

The Lukan author's view of the Holy Spirit can be very helpful for today's church. Many congregations in the long-established denominations do not have a clear view of the Spirit, and they do not talk or think much about it. Some congregations have a low quotient of religious experience, that is, they do not feel a strong sense of the *transcendent*. Indeed, some congregations are lethargic. They carry on business as usual without a vital sense of animation or of serving a purpose beyond maintaining their own institutional security.

Luke's permeating emphasis on the Holy Spirit urges the Christian community to be alert for its presence, leading, and empowerment. Luke–Acts invites Christian communities today to be aware that the Spirit is attempting to stir the community to vital interior religious experience and to mission beyond the community. The latter is an indication of the presence of the former. The former is power for the latter.

On the other hand, some churches today have an intense awareness of the Holy Spirit that results in vivid interior religious life and dramatic expressions of the Spirit (e.g., speaking in tongues), but do not witness more broadly to the movement of the realm of God. They may not witness to God's unconditional love and call for justice to restore broken relationships and community in the social world beyond the congregation.

It poses a problem that we cannot observe the Holy Spirit through laboratory-like empirical methods, yet we need to be able to identify the presence and movement of the Spirit. The author of Luke–Acts implies some criteria that help us name whether an experience or prompting might be the result of the Holy Spirit. The Holy Spirit induces the energizing awareness of the God of Israel as known through the First Testament and Jesus Christ. The Holy Spirit seeks to restore the divided human family by bringing together persons and groups who have been separated, as, for example, through the Gentile mission. When a person or movement seeks to disintegrate further the human family or the created world, we can usually conclude that such movements do not originate with the Spirit. The Spirit leads to the restoration of other aspects of this broken world, for example, through providing for the poor, helping relieve the rich of the burden of their wealth, and restoring the place of women in the Christian community and in the wider world. The Spirit is likely to be the animating power where such developments take place. The work of the Spirit is always consistent with God's unconditional love for all and God's call for justice for all.

One of the most characteristic works of the Spirit in Luke–Acts is to enlarge the community's vision of the cosmic restoration. Indeed, the Lukan author says explicitly that God is never, in any time or place, without witness for doing good (Acts 14:17) and that God even provides for the well-being of people who do not recognize God (Acts 17:24–28). It follows that the Spirit is at work for restoration in circumstances outside the Christian community. The preacher is called to help the Christian community recognize such situations and to join them.

The hermeneutic of analogy can help the preacher relate the positive emphasis on the Spirit in Luke–Acts to today's situation. For example, how is the Spirit filling us in ways that are analogous to those that the author of Luke–Acts describes? Where, in the contemporary world, is the Spirit forming communities who witness in the patterns of Jesus and the church in Acts? Where is the Spirit leading our communities to welcome the contemporary equivalent of Gentiles and empowering other signs of the restoration?

One aspect of the Jewish, and specifically Lukan, perspective on the Spirit troubles me. At one level, the Spirit is omnipresent. It breathes life into the creation. Without the Spirit, existence would cease. At another level, this tradition speaks as if the Spirit is poured out in extra measure on selected people or groups at selected times. Thus, there are times that the Spirit could pour forth, but does not. If the Spirit has the capacity to fill and restore, why would it be withheld in the face of profound need? If the Spirit is deliberately held back when it could help restore, then God and the Spirit are unjust and unloving.

I maintain, instead, that the Spirit is truly omnipresent—doing all that it can do. It perpetually wills to fill and renew. However, our consciousness of the Spirit is limited. Things get in the way of our perception of the fullness of the Spirit's presence and activity. From time to time (often for reasons that we cannot consciously articulate) we become aware of the intensity of the Spirit's presence and respond to it. From this perspective, for instance, the story of Pentecost does not narrate a time when the Spirit was actually more available than at other times, but describes a moment of heightened perception of the Spirit. The Spirit is perpetually at work as described on Pentecost, even if we do not distinguish it amid the muck of everyday living. We sometimes speak of such moments as if the Spirit "comes" (or departs), but our language is imprecise. The preacher is called to help the congregation become aware of the omnipresence and movement of the Spirit

A Sermon on the Theme of the Holy Spirit

I grew up in the church. But I cannot remember much attention being given to the Holy Spirit. In the church of my youth, a congregation of the Christian Church (Disciples of Christ) in the Ozark Mountains, I do not recall a single sermon or Bible lesson that focused in a significant way on the Spirit. In fact, I recollect the Holy Spirit being mentioned regularly only in the words of hymns and at baptism when the pastor said, "I now baptize you in the name of the Father, the Son, and the Holy Spirit." Pentecost was celebrated almost exclusively as the birthday of the church, by which we unconsciously meant the church as an institution.

In those days we often referred to the Holy Spirit as the Holy Ghost. That was a little unnerving. It conjured up images of a figure in sheets hiding behind the door.

In painful retrospect, I am also pretty sure that many of us were a little embarrassed by the congregations in town that were known as Holy Spirit churches. I grew up in the 1950s and 1960s, before air conditioning was the norm. After our Sunday evening service, we would sometimes drive by these churches. They had their windows open, and you could see what was happening. The music was not the standard pipe organ fare as at our congregation. They had piano, guitars, a violin (we called it a fiddle), even a tambourine. The people danced and spoke in tongues. As the service neared its climax, some people would be slain in the Spirit; they would stand up, get stiff as a board, and drop straight over. If such phenomena were the standard work of the Holy Spirit, I was one youth who was glad to keep a certain distance from it.

Like the other young people in our church, I was a Bible reader as a young person, and I read the gospel of Luke and the book of Acts several times. Acts, in particular, was a favorite in our church because we wanted to be like that early Christian community.

But sometimes we see only what we are prepared to see. I was completely unaware of the fact that the Holy Spirit permeates Luke and Acts until I took a course on Luke in seminary and our teacher referred to it as the gospel of the Holy Spirit.

Sure enough, Luke has almost as many references to the Spirit as Matthew and Mark combined. And Acts has almost that many more. Even more important than word count is the fact that Luke describes or implies the Spirit present at the most significant events in the narrative—birth, baptism, temptation, and first sermon of Jesus, Pentecost, in confrontations with the local authorities, beginning the Gentile mission, leading Paul to Rome.

Why the fuss? Why so much Holy Spirit in Luke and Acts? The Spirit is a divine representative who fills people with power and who energizes the restoration of the world. The Holy Spirit is similar to electricity that flows from God into communities and events, filling them with the awareness of the holy presence and bringing them alive to witness to the world that God wants. Furthermore, Luke tells the story in such a way as to suggest that the Spirit works in the church and world today very much as it worked in the worlds of Jesus and the early Christian communities.

The Spirit is responsible for the birth of Jesus. The angel says to Mary, "The Holy Spirit will come upon you, and the power of the Most High will overshadow you; therefore the child to be born will be holy" (Lk. 1:35). This language recalls an important work of the Holy Spirit from the First Testament. At the creation of the world, God brooded over a deep, primeval sea. This sea represents the power of chaos. Chaos is incredible but unfocused energy. Imagine an ocean whose waves are in a tumult, beating against themselves. The Spirit preserves the chaos so that it does not destroy itself. Then God works with the Spirit to help turn the pointless energy of chaos into elements that become community.

At the time of Luke, the world had become a chaos. Roman military presence. Heavy taxation. Idolatry. Poverty. People selling themselves into slavery to pay their debts. The temple in Jerusalem destroyed. Conflict between traditional authorities and Christian Jews. Conflict within the church. Sound familiar? Our world is in a kind of chaos. Multiple forms of exploitation. People worshiping the idols of wealth, success, money, power, gender, race, and sexual orientation. Poverty. Conflict between the church and culture. Conflict within congregations and among Christian movements.

The Spirit moves through Jesus to help re-create the world. Out of the chaos, the Spirit seeks to bring forth a community in which all are valued and free, and in the kinds of relationships that God wants. The Spirit is still moving through Jesus Christ and the church to create such a world.

When Jesus is baptized in the Jordan, he is filled with the Spirit. Jesus is the paradigm of how the Spirit works in the world. The expression "filled" is key. Like water splashing out of a pump and into a pitcher, the Spirit fills a community with the awareness of the Holy, the Great Providential Other. The filling is not an end itself. As water in the pitcher is to refresh thirsty mouths, to wash dirty hands, to pour onto plants to help them grow, so the Spirit is power for mission, in particular, witnessing to the reign of God. Can you feel it pulsing in the world around? Pulsing in you?

In his first sermon at Nazareth, Jesus portrays Spirit-filled life by saying that the Spirit moves through him to bring good news to the poor, to proclaim release to the captives and recovery of sight to the blind, to free the oppressed and to proclaim the year of the Lord's favor.

Sure enough, Jesus provides for the needs of the poor—feeding the hungry in the wilderness and prompting Zacchaeus and other wealthy people to share their money with the poor. Jesus releases people from the grip of demons. Jesus heals the blind and many others. These actions point beyond themselves. They represent the restoration of the community to God's purposes. And they take place under the impulse of the Spirit.

The reference to the year of the Lord's favor recalls the Jubilee—that time every fifty years in Israel when debts would be forgiven, slaves would be freed, and land would revert to its original owners. The ruptures of community of the last fifty years were canceled and the community could begin again. Luke has in mind a *cosmic* Jubilee when God re-creates the whole world so that every relationship in every circumstance embodies God's love and justice. This process of transformation is underway.

However, this gospel is harshly realistic. Some people and powers are so entrenched in the present that they will not relinquish power. They think that cosmic renewal threatens their power. So they resist. Satan. The demons. Local authorities. The Romans. In the end, they conspire to put Jesus death. But... the Spirit sustains Jesus in his suffering. At the very end, Jesus yields himself to God.

Just as the Spirit is poured out upon Jesus, so it was poured out at Pentecost. The church provided for the poor by making their material resources available for the whole community. The early Christians released people from demonic possession. And three times, when disciples were imprisoned, God opened the prison doors, and they walked out free. The disciples healed the lame, and yes, even raised the dead. The Spirit of the cosmic regeneration worked through them. In perhaps the most dramatic example of the manifestation of the year of the Lord's favor, the Holy Spirit led the church to welcome Gentiles into their companionship. The cosmic Jubilee gives the whole human family a new start. And that is the work of the Holy Spirit.

Yes, the disciples also encountered opposition. In Jerusalem, they were hauled into court. On the missionary journeys, local authorities harrassed them, and crowds tried to mob them. Stephen was stoned but in the Spirit yielded himself just as Jesus did. About a third of the book of Acts tells the story of Paul's arrest and various trials as he made his way to Rome. But throughout, the Holy Spirit sustained. Indeed, the Spirit even gave the disciples and Paul the words with which to respond to their accusers.

What do we have in this story? A picture of the Spirit-filled life. A spirit who fills, who empowers for actions of renewal, who brings the word of God to expression, who is an assuring presence in times of struggle. This Spirit is still active today.

Every semester in a class that I teach on introduction to preaching, we watch a videotape of a sermon from Charles Adams, minister of Hartford Baptist Church in Detroit. An African American with a Ph.D. in social ethics from Harvard,

Pastor Adams is sometimes called the "Harvard Whooper." As the sermon begins, our European American students are typically fascinated by Adams' profound sense of spiritual presence, by the magnetic quality of his voice, by his remarkable use of language. But soon, these students become unaware of style and mannerisms and are carried in the flow of the sermon as it builds in intensity. Adams climaxes with that powerful pattern of intonation that we call whooping or moaning.

Watching Dr. Adams preach on videotape, my classes can feel the energy of the Holy Spirit in the sermon and in the congregation. They feel the Spirit filling the preacher and moving through the message. The class members comment on it every time.

But the ecstatic overflow is not an end in itself. Hartford Baptist Church is located in the center of urban Detroit. In the midst of the sermon, Pastor Adams describes a remarkable project sponsored by the congregation. They bought thirteen acres, much of it formerly occupied by crack houses, liquor stores, and other businesses that drain the community of money and human potential. They have cleared the land and are building a Super K-Mart, plus many other stores and restaurants and parking for more than one thousand cars.

At first I couldn't believe my ears. A Baptist K-Mart (my name, not his)? Selling discount underwear for God? Yet, Adams explains, this store will provide seven hundred jobs in a neighborhood where unemployment is 40 percent. Those people will not only immediately benefit but will become part of an economic power base to help provide other jobs in the neighborhood.

The store will provide neighborhood access to goods that people now have to drive at least half an hour to find. People who don't have a car (and many people in the ghetto do not) ride a bus for more than an hour one-way to get such things. This development will contain an optometrist (what was that about opening the eyes of the blind?), a dentist, and several other services not presently found there. It will have a bank with reasonable lending rates. Not quite the Jubilee, but it does provide access to capital. The development will pour hundreds of thousands of new dollars into the tax revenues of Detroit.

When their representatives speak at city council, others will pay more attention. This complex will provide a hallway of clean, warm telephone booths indoors so that people who don't have phones can make calls without standing in the cold Detroit winter. And yes, discount underwear is a blessing for children who have never had new underwear.

Charles Adams is clear that the Baptist K-Mart is not the reign of God. But it is an immediate way of helping a specific neighborhood experience something of the renewal that God has in mind for the whole world.

At first my mind was blown by the prospect of a Baptist K-Mart. Blue-light specials for God. But something else is even more mind-blowing. How many congregations do I know that have the vision even to conceive such a possibility? How many congregations that I know would act in such a way? (My congregation engaged in an all-out, two-month financial campaign just to get a new sound system.)

Where does the Detroit flock get this vision? This power? Where does the congregation get the power to sign its name to a multimillion-dollar loan to begin this project? From the Holy Spirit.

The Spirit brought Jesus into the world. At his baptism Jesus was filled with the Spirit. The story of Jesus demonstrates the Spirit-filled life. Jesus promises this Spirit to the disciples. When they receive it, they are imbued with power that both fills them and stretches them. A Gentile mission? A Baptist K-Mart?

The remarkable promise of Luke is that the Holy Spirit is still in the world, seeking to fill us with the awareness of the divine, seeking to re-create our world so that it becomes a place of love and justice for all. The Spirit works whether we notice it or not. But when we consciously receive it, we feel its presence in the depths of our being. We are empowered for possibilities in life and community that we would have thought beyond our reach. I yearn to be open to this Spirit. I yearn for our church to be open to this Spirit. Don't you?

CHAPTER 5

Preaching on the Great Reunion of the Human Community

Luke–Acts anticipates the day when the divided human family will be reunited in a great eschatological community. Jesus and the church witness to and facilitate aspects of this reunion. Preachers sometimes consider this topic under separate subheadings such as fellowship with tax collectors and sinners, relationship with Samaritans, and mission to the Gentiles. While each of these subtopics has its own nuances, they cohere around the theme of the regathering of the human community that takes place in the realm of God.

In this chapter, I sketch Jewish attitudes toward Gentiles, Samaritans, sinners, tax collectors, and others who are part of the ingathering of the scattered elements of the human family in Luke's corpus. The core of the chapter follows the path of reunion in Luke–Acts. After some observations on the continuing value of this perspective for the contemporary Christian community, the chapter ends with a sermon.

A Jewish View of the Broken Human Community

The theological world of Luke–Acts presumes a broad story of how the human community came to be segregated into different groups and of how the vocation of Israel fits into the wider human family. From the apocalyptic and other perspectives, God created one human family with Eve and Adam as its progenitors (e.g., Lk. 3:38; Acts 17:24–26). God intended human beings to live together as a harmonious community.

However, after the fall (Gen. 3:9–16), enmity immediately erupted among human beings (Gen. 4:1ff.). When strife reached monumental levels, God destroyed the world and began with another human nucleus (Gen. 6:1–9:28), from whom descended subsequent generations (Gen. 10:1–11; cf. Acts 2:5–13). However, because these groups banded together to build the tower of Babel, God cursed them (Gen. 11:1–9; cf. Acts 2:5–13; 10:44–48).

After God's attempts to bless all human beings as a single family went awry, God changed strategy. God decided to bless the whole of humankind by calling one human family who would serve as the channel of blessing: Sarah and Abraham and their descendents (Gen. 12:2–3).

Human beings outside the Jewish community came to be known as "Gentiles." They are sometimes referred to as the "peoples" or "nations" (though some contexts suggest that these expressions occasionally include Israel). An important strand of the First Testament continues to stress that God intends to bless Gentiles. For instance, in Isaiah 42:6 God gives Israel as "a covenant to the people, a light to the nations" (cf. Isa. 49:6; Ex. 19:3–6; Ps. 72:17; Isa. 52:13–53:12, especially 4–6, 10–12). The books of Jonah and Ruth stress God's love for Gentiles.

A spirit of openness to the Gentiles is found in much Jewish literature (e.g., Ex. 15:11; Deut. 10:17–18; 1 Kings 8:41–43; 2 Kings 5:1–19; Ps. 47:2; Dan. 2:47; Wis. 5:18; Sir. 35:15–16). My colleague Calvin L. Porter describes the Septuagint as "Gentile-friendly." Some Jewish people conclude that Gentiles who do not convert to Judaism can be righteous by obeying the Noachic laws (i.e., laws that some Jewish teachers thought were implicit in the story of Noah). These laws prohibit blasphemy, idolatry, adultery, bloodshed, robbery, and eating the flesh of live animals. They call for justice. The Lukan author clearly moves in this stream (Acts 15:28–29).[1]

To be sure, Gentiles are often idolaters. They rage against God and against Israel. They practice multiple forms of injustice, abuse, and violence. The Gentiles cause Israel to suffer. But God still seeks to bless them.

Some Jewish theologians foresee Gentiles rejoining the Jewish family in serving the God of Israel (e.g., Isa. 2:2–4; 25:6–8;

45:22; 51:3–5; 60:1–7; 61:5–8; cf. Mic. 4:1–4; Zech. 8:20–23).
Enoch describes the coming of Gentiles to God as part of the
cosmic restoration:

> And all children of the people will become righteous,
> and all nations shall worship and bless me; and they
> will all prostrate themselves to me. And the earth shall
> be cleansed from all pollution, from all sin, and from
> all plague, and from all suffering; and it shall not hap-
> pen again that I shall send [these] upon the earth from
> generation to generation forever.[2] (*1 Enoch* 10:18–22)

The end time (the great reunion) will be similar to the beginning time (when the whole human community dwelt together
as one).[3]

Christians sometimes speak in caricature of Jewish attitudes
toward Gentiles. For instance, students often mention "the ha-
tred of Jews for Gentiles." While tensions did exist between
Jewish and Gentile worlds, these people often lived side by
side on a friendly basis. At its best, Jewish theology interprets
Judaism as mission for Gentiles.

Jewish and Samaritan peoples emerged from the same family. Prior to the exile, the Samaritans were a conventional Jewish group. During the exile, the Samaritans emerged as a group
distinct from conventional Jewish people. They believed that
Moses commanded worship on Mount Gerizim. To them, only
the five books of Moses were sacred scripture. The Samaritans
developed their own tradition of interpreting these books (e.g.,
Adam was made from the dust of Mount Gerizim). They anticipated that Moses would be the eschatological prophet. Some
Jewish people regarded Samaritans as "half-breeds."

Samaritan and Jewish people frequently lived near one another in relative peace. Jewish people from Galilee regularly
passed through Samaria. However, relationships were sometimes acrimonious. For instance, according to Josephus, some
Samaritans scattered human bones in the temple during one
Passover.[4]

Preachers often comment, "We all are sinners." This statement is true in the generic sense. However, in Jewish antiquity
the term *sinners* had a more specific meaning. The term is "best

translated 'the wicked,' and it refers to those who sinned willfully and heinously and who did not repent."[5] Some sinners held sinful jobs. For example, moneylenders engaged in willful sin by charging interest. However, sinners could flagrantly disavow God by violating covenantal community in multiple ways.

Sinners were an active threat to social stability as God intended it through the practice of covenant in community. Consequently, sinners were often excluded from social relationships except insofar as people had to deal with them. Luke presumes this understanding of sinner. Through repentance (which sometimes included making restitution), sinners could be restored to fullness of participation in community life.

A tax collector was a Jewish person who worked for a Gentile official who was responsible for collecting taxes for Rome and its various governmental extensions. Interpreters often speak of tax collectors as quislings because they cooperated with the forces of Roman occupation. Tax collectors could overcharge taxes assessed on the local population. Tax collectors were an active threat to covenantal community as they gouged the people and drained the community of valuable economic resources. However, tax collectors could repent, make restitution, and return to participation in the community.

The Reunion of the Human Family in Luke–Acts

Luke–Acts portrays the restoration of the human family now underway through Jesus Christ and the ministry of the church. While Luke portends the Gentile mission, Jesus has only a handful of contacts with Gentiles. However, Jesus' welcome of sinners and tax collectors is the pattern for the church's welcome of Gentiles in Acts. The actions of Jesus and the church prefigure the great eschatological reunion.

The Birth of Jesus Points to the Great Reunion (Lk. 1:5—2:51)

Events and sayings in connection with Jesus' birth indicate that the restoration of the human family is a major reason for the birth of Jesus. Zechariah explains that John will be a part of the light breaking for those in darkness (Lk. 1:78–79; cf.

Isa. 42:7; 60:1–3). Darkness, a multivalent symbol in Jewish writings, describes both the captivity of Israel and Gentile existence. Gentiles now come to know the tender mercy of God much as the Jewish community does.

The shepherds are the first persons outside the immediate family to receive the news of Jesus' birth (Lk. 2:8–20). Many people in antiquity regarded shepherds with suspicion. As a group they were not "sinners," but they were regarded as rough. Working in isolation from the rest of the community, they were reputed to steal the best sheep (e.g., Gen. 30:25–43). The fact that the angels visit the shepherds before anyone else indicates the strength of the motif of the restoration of the human community. This thrust is reinforced by the news that Jesus' birth is "for all the people" (Lk. 2:10).

Simeon similarly interprets the significance of Jesus' birth. The news that will comfort Israel is that God is preparing for the salvation (i.e., the universal restoration) of all people. This salvation is a light to the Gentiles and the glory of Israel (Lk. 2:29–32).

Jesus' Relationships and Teachings Prefigure the Great Reunion (3:1—23:56)

John the Baptist prepares the way for Jesus. When the Lukan author interprets the ministry of John the Baptist with Isaiah 40:3–5, he points to the great reunion as a part of the cosmic renewal: "*All flesh* shall see the salvation of God" (Lk. 3:6; Isa. 40:5).

The genealogy of Jesus traces Jesus' ancestry directly to Adam, thus connecting Jesus with God's purposes at the very beginning of history when humankind was a single community (Lk. 3:38). All the children of Eve and Adam will be restored.

The great reunion is a significant theme in Jesus' first sermon at Nazareth. Jesus reads from Isaiah 61:1–2 and 58:6 announcing that the universal renewal is now manifest (Lk. 4:16–21). The larger context of Isaiah would echo in the ancient listener's memory. Isaiah 61:4–5, 10–11 speak specifically of Gentiles feeding the flocks of Israel and of righteousness being manifested in the nations. Jesus offers two illustrations of this renewal. Elijah was sent to a Gentile widow in Zarephath. Elisha healed Namaan, not only a Gentile but also a general in the Syrian army, which was sometimes an enemy of Israel (Lk. 4:24–28).

Jesus calls a tax collector named Levi to follow him, that is, to become a disciple (Lk. 5:27–28). Soon Jesus is known as a friend of tax collectors and sinners and partakes of the first of several meals with them (5:29–32; cf. 7:34; 15:1–2; 19:1–10). Scholars point out that these meals enact a miniature version of the eschatological banquet when the ruptures in the human community are healed. Tax collectors, sinners, and others who repent are welcome participants in the movement toward restoration.

In a story that echoes 2 Kings 5:1–14 (the healing of Namaan), a centurion sends a delegation to ask Jesus to heal the slave. While Jesus is still far away from the slave, the centurion says that Jesus needs only to speak the word from afar for the slave to be healed (Lk. 7:1–10). Jesus exclaims that he (Jesus) has not found such faith even in Israel. Jesus speaks. The slave is healed. The realm of God is manifested in behalf of a Gentile commander. Even a Roman centurion can be a model of response to the restoration.

A woman who is described as a sinner is forgiven (Lk. 7:36–50). On the way to Jerusalem, Jesus makes an overture to Samaritans (9:51–56). The parable of the good Samaritan urges listeners to recognize that Samaritans can be faithful to the realm of God while priest and Levite can turn away (10:25–37). A Samaritan returns to thank Jesus for healing, while nine conventional Jewish lepers do not (17:11–19). These Samaritans are models for covenantal relationships.

Jesus says that "people will come from east and west, from north and south, and will eat in the [dominion] of God" (Lk. 13:22–30). These directions represent the ends of the earth (cf. Acts 1:8). The larger narrative context makes it likely that the author of Luke–Acts envisions the coming of Gentiles to the eschatological banquet (e.g., Isa. 25:6–8).

In a parable, the initial three guests refuse the invitation to the great dinner (a type of eschatological banquet). The host then sends the slaves to the streets and eventually to the "roads and lanes" (Lk. 14:15–24). This language alludes to those who are outside Israel, that is, Gentiles (e.g., Deut. 32:21).

Jesus tells some of the most famous parables in Luke in response to the fact that some Pharisees and scribes grumble (as in Num. 11:1–15; 14:1–4) that Jesus welcomes tax collectors and sinners and eats with them (Lk. 15:1–2). The parables of the lost sheep and the lost coin make the point that such persons have a place in the community of the restoration when they repent (Lk. 15:3–10). The parable of the parent and the two children elaborates the same lesson but applies it specifically to Gentiles. The younger heir makes himself the same as a Gentile, yet after repentance, God welcomes this younger heir to the eschatological banquet (15:11–24).

A tax collector becomes the model of humility and repentance (Lk. 18:9–14). Soon, Zacchaeus welcomes Jesus, repents of his extortions, and seeks to make restitution by paying back four times as much as he had defrauded (19:1–10). Zacchaeus models repentance and restitution.

Luke does not romanticize Gentiles, sinners, or tax collectors. Both Jewish and Gentile people collude to put Jesus to death. However, Jesus welcomes into the restored world one of the criminals crucified next to him when that criminal moves in the direction of repentance (23:39–43). A Roman centurion confesses Jesus' innocence, thereby ending the Gentile presence in Luke on a positive note (23:47).

The Commission to Witness to the Reunion of the Human Family (Lk. 24:1—Acts 1:26)

The resurrection of Jesus demonstrates that the time of the regeneration of the cosmos is underway (Lk. 24:1–43). Before ascending, the risen Jesus explains the vocation of the church: to preach repentance and forgiveness of sins in the name of Jesus *to all nations*, that is, to the Gentiles, beginning with Jerusalem. This ministry is the goal of the teachings of Moses, the prophets, and the writings.

This commission is reinforced in Acts 1. The disciples ask Jesus when he is going to restore the dominion of Israel. Jesus reframes their request to include the Gentile mission, as if to suggest that the inclusion of the Gentiles is part of the restoration of Israel (Acts 1:6–7). The church is to carry the message of the realm of God from Jerusalem and Judea through Samaria and then to the ends of the earth (Acts 1:8).

The Movement toward the Gentiles from Judea and Samaria (Acts 2:1—8:40)

In Acts the news of God's ingathering realm goes from Jerusalem through Samaria to the ends of the earth, that is, to the Gentiles. At Pentecost, the Holy Spirit falls on a Christian Jewish congregation at Jerusalem to empower them (Acts 2:1–47). The national boundaries within which the Jewish people live, such as Parthians, Medes, Elamites, and so on, are superseded by the restoration of common identity in the Spirit (2:1–4). The dissolution of human community at Babel is now reversed (Gen.11:1–9). Peter quotes Joel 2:28 to specify that the Spirit is poured *"upon all flesh"* (Acts 2:17; cf. 10:44–48; Lk. 3:4–6).

Peter grounds the mission in God's promises to Sarah and Abraham (Acts 3:25–26; cf. 3:13). These promises implicitly invoke the reunion of the human family, for God's promise to the first couple was that their family would become a channel of blessing for all (Gen. 12:1–3). Stephen also invokes this memory (Acts 7:2–8, 16, especially 17, 32). The God of Israel is, by definition, the God of all (e.g., Acts 7:49–50).

The realistic portrayal of the Gentiles continues as Peter points out that rage is a characteristic of Gentile life. Indeed, Gentiles colluded in the death of Jesus (3:23–31).

Just as the risen Jesus said, the mission moves through Judea and toward Samaria (8:1b–3). Samaritans welcome the gospel (8:4–8). A famous Samaritan magician, Simon, is baptized. However, Simon's role in the story is a cautionary tale (8:9–25). While Luke has earlier used Samaritans as surprising positive models (Lk. 10:25–37; 17:11–17), Simon now reminds us that Samaritans are also ambiguous. Reunion must be joined with adequate nurture in the way of discipleship.

The news of the restoration also moves toward the ends of the earth when the Spirit leads Philip to the chariot of the Ethiopian eunuch (Acts 8:25–40). As a eunuch this African has a limited sense of future because he has no posterity. However, in line with the promise of Isaiah 56:3–5, the restoration means that this eunuch is no longer "a dry tree." The eunuch is a member of a community whose posterity includes all the children of Eve and Adam.

Gentiles Are Welcomed in the Community Witnessing to the Restoration (Acts 9:1—28:32)

The manifestation of the restoration of the Gentiles comes to direct expression from two complementary sources (Paul in Acts 9:1–19; Peter in Acts 10:1–11:18). Despite the credentials in support of the restoration of Gentiles that the Lukan author has developed, the church is initially conflicted over it and must settle the difficulty at the apostolic council (Acts 15). The rest of Acts tells the story of Paul's taking the gospel on a route that leads to Rome.

The risen Jesus calls Paul to be a missionary to the Gentiles (Acts 9:1–19; cf. 22:3–21; 26:4–23). The author uses a vision to impress upon the listeners the authenticity of the content of the vision. Paul had been an opponent of the restoration of the Gentiles, but God called Paul in language very similar to the calls of Isaiah and Jeremiah (Isa. 49:1; Jer. 1:5, 10; 50:25; Acts 9:15; cf. 22:14–15, 20; 26:17–18, 23). The restoration of the Gentiles is in direct continuity with these prophetic ministries.

Peter (archetypal representative of Christian Judaism) and Cornelius (centurion God-fearer) are given visions that bring them together, along with some other Gentiles (Acts 10:1–33). Peter explains that "God shows no partiality, but in every nation anyone who fears [God] and does what is right is acceptable to [God]" (10:34–35). When the Holy Spirit pours out on this audience, the listener realizes that the eschatological ingathering has now reached the Gentile community, for the Gentiles have the same standing before God and have received the same Spirit as the Jewish community.

Almost immediately, some early Christians question the validity of this experience. Yet Peter asserts, "God has given even to the Gentiles the repentance that leads to life" (Acts 11:18). Other Gentiles are soon added (11:19–26, especially 20). When Paul preaches at Antioch of Pisidia, he brings the memory of Sarah and Abraham onto the horizon. The church is to do its part as "light for the Gentiles" (13:13–52, especially 38–39, 46–47; cf. Isa. 49:6).

The apostolic council deals with the insistence of some Christian Jewish leaders that Gentile converts should be circumcised and otherwise take on the Jewish life. In the previous chapter, I discussed the deliberations of the council (p. 79). It is enough now to point out that the directive of the council to the Gentiles partakes of the openness to Gentiles we have seen in elements of Judaism mentioned earlier.

While I do not claim that the conclusions of the council are directly related to the Noachic commandments, the requirements set forth by the council are in the spirit of the commandments. The Gentiles are to "abstain from what has been offered to idols and from blood and from what is strangled and from fornication" (Acts 15:29, author's trans.). The converts are to distance themselves from behavior associated with the idolatry and immorality characteristic of Gentiles and are to move in the direction of life practices consistent with Judaism. Converts are to be de-paganized and modestly Judaized. Gentiles become full participants in the church's witness to the universal restoration by repentance, baptism, receiving the Holy Spirit, and living according to the essence of Judaism (15:28–29).

Paul makes it clear that he is not teaching Jewish people to abandon the ways of Moses, that is, to become Gentiles. On the contrary, in the spirit of Acts 15:28–29, he instructs the Gentiles to live more like the heirs of Moses (Acts 21:17–26).

In response to the troubling presence of idols in Athens, and to questions from local philosophers, the author makes his most complete theological statement on the religions of the Gentiles (Acts 17:22–31). God has made everything in heaven and on earth and breathes life into every living thing. From one ancestor, God made all people and implanted within them an intuition so that "they would grope for God" (17:23–27, author's trans.; cf. Wis. 13:1–9). God is "not far from each one of us." Paul even quotes two Greek philosophers as authoritative sources for the knowledge of God (17:28). Preaching helps Gentiles correlate their religious intuition with the God of Israel and realize that God calls for repentance, for a day of universal judgment is coming (17:30–31).

While the author acknowledges positive potential in some Gentile ways, Gentile religion often results in idolatry and destructive behavior, even serving the purposes of the devil (e.g., Acts 14:8–18; 16:16–24; 19:23–39; 20:23–40). Indeed, while the Gentile mission is a goal of Acts, the author does not glorify Gentiles. Some Gentiles resist the gospel forcefully (Acts 14:1–6; 16:16–40). Gentiles collude in rejecting the gospel messengers (e.g., Acts 4:27–28; 14:5–6). Paul is delivered into the hands of Gentiles who kill him (Acts 21:11)

After Paul is falsely arrested on the charge of bringing Greeks into the temple, a tribune of the Roman cohort saves him from a vigilante death at the hands of a Jewish mob (21:27–36). God uses Roman officials to preserve Paul's life. However, Rome represents the need for Gentile restoration. Rome sent the military forces that repressed the Jewish homeland and destroyed the temple. It is a seat of flagrant idolatry. Roman officials or their surrogates repeatedly examine Paul's case and declare his innocence, but they are morally spineless and do nothing to prevent his inexorable journey. Rome is responsible for Paul's martyrdom.

That God sends the gospel to Rome as part of sending it to the "ends of the earth" (Acts 1:8) indicates the strength of God's resolve to restore the whole human family. God wishes for Rome (and all that it represents) to repent and be renewed. God will not allow anything to stand in the way of the gospel's reaching Rome–not Jewish opposition, not Roman judicial incompetence, not even nature (27:13–28:6). Acts climaxes with Paul's witnessing to the restoration in the heart of Rome (28:11–31).

As Luke–Acts ends, Paul stresses that God will continue to work toward the great reunion of the human family through the Gentile mission (Acts 28:29). The narrative is designed to inspire the reader with the confidence that this reunion is God's will.

The Great Reunion of the Human Community Today

Luke's two volumes remind today's church that we are called to witness to the great reunion of the human family. Since most Christians today are Gentiles, the first effect of this theme in the life of the church should be to prompt our thanks and praise to the God of Israel for making it possible for us to know the divine love, grace, *hesed*, and mercy through Jesus Christ.

Furthermore, today's Christian community should welcome persons who are today's equivalents of Gentiles, Samaritans, tax collectors, and sinners into full participation in the community that is to witness to the renewed world.

I make hermeneutical use of the notion of Gentile at two levels. At one level, Gentiles are simply all who are not Jewish. Many Gentiles in the world today need to know that, through Jesus Christ, they are loved and welcomed by the God of Israel into a community in which all relationships are renewed.

At another level, Gentiles are those who are different, and those whose differences cause us to keep them at a distance. The hermeneutic of analogy helps us see that contemporary Christians sometimes regard people with reservations that are similar to those with which some Christian Jewish congregations regarded the Gentile mission in the first century. Luke's emphasis on the great reunion of the human family prompts us to witness to the fact that God, through the Holy Spirit, makes it possible for such distant (and sometimes suspicious) relationships to be replaced by community, support, even intimacy.

Many congregations today are composed mainly of persons who are similar in race, gender relationships, economic status, social class, philosophy, and politics. Contemporary Christian communities frequently reflect the same tensions as the wider world. By contrast, a Lukan church is to embody the eschatological human community by embracing tax collector, sinner, Samaritan, Gentile.

Even more striking, tax collectors and sinners have been engaged in activities that are flagrantly disobedient and that threaten the well-being of the community, and they may even have been a threat to it. The church is not to stand over such persons with an air of moral superiority but is to fellowship with them and extend the opportunity for restoration to them. When they repent, the church is to welcome them.

The author of Luke–Acts does more than urge us to establish community with Gentiles, Samaritans, tax collectors, and sinners. He sometimes uses these figures as models of faithfulness. What can our churches *learn* about God and the faithful life from today's tax collectors, sinners, Samaritans, and Gentiles?

The Lukan author further pushes the contemporary Christian community to recognize that God is at work in all times and places. Indeed, God is universal and impartial. Persons outside Judaism and Christianity can know something of God, can receive God's blessing, and can even make a faithful witness. Christian missionaries explain, "In past generations, [God] allowed all the nations to follow their own ways; *yet [God] has never left [Godself] without a witness in doing good*–giving you rains from heaven and fruitful seasons, and filling you with food and your hearts with joy" (Acts 14:16–17, author's trans.). Paul asserts that Gentiles have some positive knowledge of God as a result of nature and even Greek philosophy and religion (17:22–34). Some Gentiles intuit the divine through an "unknown god." Paul cites the Greek poet and philosopher Epimenides as an authority (17:28a; 26:14). The Lukan author thus pushes the Christian community to be on the alert for the many manifestations of God's presence in the world, including surprising arenas. Since God is omnipresent, we are pressed to ask not only what other religions might have in common with Judaism and Christianity, but also how they might instruct us.

A Sermon on the Theme of the Great Reunion of the Human Community

My extended family is now spread over Missouri, Oklahoma, Indiana, Texas, Florida, Georgia, Colorado, New Jersey, and the Philippines. To the astonishment of many of our friends, our family has a big reunion for a long weekend every July.

Sometimes I can easily tell we are related. I am an only child, but when I am with these cousins I see and hear aspects of myself. I hear my own speech patterns in other people, observe my own mannerisms, or recognize my own weaknesses.

At the same time, we are quite different. Most of my Oklahoma cousins were on state championship athletic teams. I have so little eye-hand coordination I was once asked not to try out for a grade-school basketball team. Some of my relatives hold political and theological views that are diametrically opposed to mine. The family is largely European American, but through marriage and adoption it now includes African Americans, Native Americans, and children who are transracial. Regardless of the differences, I have a deep sense of connection with these people. We come from the same roots. Some of the same life factors are at work in all of us.

For the reunion we rent a church camp. On the night the reunion begins, cars pull into the parking lot with horns blasting. People run out of the dormitories and embrace and shout and laugh. Passing around pictures. Telling stories. Eating only things that are made with generous quantities of chocolate. Swimming all night. Water balloon fights. One thoughtless Fourth of July we had a bottle rocket war. Yes, using garbage can lids as shields and shooting at one another with bottle rockets. The way my children remember that event, life could never get any better.

I practically never see these relatives during the year. But they are a part of who I am. All year long our household talks about the reunion and looks forward to it.

Luke envisions a great reunion similar to this one. People will come from north and south and east and west to eat at table in the reign of God. Luke has in mind a reunion not just of blood kin, but of the whole human community.

Speaking of "family" in this way can be a problem. The very use of the term *family* seems to raise the hand of superiority over households made up of mom, dad, two model children, a minivan, and a shaggy dog and to discount other kinds of households. Some people feel excluded by family talk. Some families are dysfunctional. Some families are toxic. Sometimes we need to leave our families for our own growth or safety. Nevertheless, my experience of family reunion is so positive, I come back to this way of talking. Nearly everyone that I know participates in some community that is supportive and life giving. I hope that people for whom family is a negative category can transfer my use of "family" to their primary communities. When re-gathering, nearly all of us experience reunion that enables us to identify with Luke.

The word *reunion* catches Luke's spirit. Ever since the tower of Babel, the human race has been divided into groups that do not support one another as fully as they could. In Luke's world, the basic division in the human race was between Gentile and Jewish peoples. These peoples divide further into national and ethnic groups. Parthians. Medes. Elamites. Each competes for power, control, and wealth.

In Bible study groups, people often ask, "Who are Gentiles?" The answer: everyone who isn't Jewish. I am Gentile. Chances are, so are you. The most important Gentile problem: idolatry. Left by themselves, Gentiles make deities of rocks, sticks, pieces of scrap metal, even ourselves. Look in the mirror and see your own god. The gods we worship determine the kind of world in which we live. If I worship something that is nothing more than myself slightly magnified, then my world is shaped by little more than my own prejudices, jealousies, greed, suspicion.

My colleague Clark Williamson recalls some of our Gentile ancestors who, for worship, painted themselves blue and bayed at the moon. Very edifying. Today, of course, we don't paint ourselves blue. But we do set up our altars of race, ethnicity, nationality, economic status, and social class. Idols lead to a world of envy, suspicion, greed, feelings of superiority, animosity, and violence. The human family is scattered.

Jewish people worship the God of Israel. But this God is no parochial deity. God is the universal sovereign who transcends all and wills love and justice for all peoples.

I sometimes hear Christians speak as if the Jewish people had an overbearing sense of superiority toward Gentiles. We need to put reverse thrust on that idea. According to Genesis, the purpose of Judaism is to help Gentiles. God says to Sarah and Abraham, "I will bless you…so that you will be a blessing…In you all the families of the earth shall be blessed" (Gen. 12:2–3). Israel is chosen not for privilege, but for the special purpose of being a means through whom the Gentiles could know the fullness of life and community that God intends. To be blessed is to be a part of a community in which all members treat one another with love and justice.

According to the Christian community, through Jesus Christ Gentiles can enjoy reunion with the God of Israel, with Jewish people, with one another, and with the pathway to blessing.

Luke traces the genealogy of Jesus in such a way as to remind us that we all are descended from the first two parents, Eve and Adam. One of the purposes of Jesus' ministry is to rekindle this awareness, so that we can reclaim one another as sisters and brothers. Jesus welcomes sinners and tax collectors into community. He heals the slave of a Roman centurion. Immediately before ascending, Jesus commissions the church: "Repentance and forgiveness of sins is to be proclaimed to all nations."

Under the power of the Holy Spirit, the early church became a community in which Jewish Christians, God-fearers, Samaritans, and Gentiles came together in response to the God of Israel and in which they became fully supportive of one another. The Gentiles take their idols off the mantel in the family room. Once greedy, they now share their wealth with the community so that there is no poverty among them. The security of knowing that one is fully accepted by the One who is ultimate takes away the need to feel superior. The communion of different kinds of people in the church points to the fully restored communion among all peoples of all times and places that will characterize the final and complete manifestation of the realm of God.

When the church becomes a community of the reunion of the scattered members of God's family, the church joins Judaism as a means whereby the blessing of the God of Israel is made known among the Gentiles.

But we must be honest. Many manifestations of the church today mirror the division and alienation of the human family. When I was growing up in the 1950s and 1960s, we often heard, "Eleven o'clock on Sunday is the most racially segregated hour of the week." Thirty years later, in many ways, it still is. But it doesn't have to be.

Sometimes we make idols of our denominations, congregations, positions, and theological formulations. Sometimes it's hard to tell the difference between the way power is exercised in the church and the way it is exercised in the Pentagon or at IBM.

I know of a congregation that refused to participate in a neighborhood food pantry because Muslims were also contributing to the pantry. By contrast, a church after the pattern of Luke and Acts is to embody the restored human community by embracing tax collectors, sinners, Samaritans, and Gentiles. We can do that because the Holy Spirit is ever present in the human midst, trying to lead us to deeper communion with one another.

When reunion occurs it is powerful. Recently I saw a twelve-minute movie titled *The Last Good War*. The opening scene is a snow-covered battlefield in Europe during the Second World War. Soldiers awkwardly bound by their thick clothes prop their guns on tree limbs to shoot. Grenades blow snow and dirt directly into the lens of the camera. The screen goes completely white with snow on the ground, and then a crimson stain of blood starts in one corner and gradually fills the screen.

The last living GI is lying on the ground, back to the the camera, fully absorbed with opening the pack of a comrade and pulling out a chocolate bar. The audience becomes aware of a German soldier, gun cocked, limping quietly toward the GI. The GI suddenly looks up, only to see the German rifle pointed directly at his head. The GI says a prayer and covers his head.

Night is falling. The scene looks so cold that I myself felt chilled. My whole body was tense, waiting for the shot. Instead, the German prods the GI into an abandoned barn. There is a handful of pieces of wood. The German makes a fire, and the two sit in its light, shivering. The German opens some food and offers it to the GI. At first suspiciously, but then hungrily, the GI eats. After a while, the German reaches in his pocket and pulls out a small Bible. In it is a picture of a young man. He holds up the picture and touches the face of the GI to indicate that the GI looks a lot like the person in the picture.

The German says, "*Bruder*." Brother. "*Tot*." Dead. "*Normandie*." They sit in silence, looking at the picture.

The GI falls asleep, and begins to shiver. The German unstraps his pack and his holsters, takes off his heavy coat, and puts it around the GI. The screen dims as the fire dies, and the theater is dark for a few moments.

Then, suddenly, bright. Next morning. The door of the barn bursts open. U.S. soldiers flood in. The GI wakes up and points to the German, now stretched out on the floor. The sergeant points a gun at the German, shouts, thumps. Nothing. The sergeant bends down and touches the German. "Dead… frozen."

Before the GI leaves, he picks up the picture, puts it into the pages of the little Bible, and tucks it into the hand of the German. He pats the body and mumbles, *"Bruder."*

So many divisions in the human community. African American. Asian American. European American. Hispanic American. Native American. Regional differences. Just for starters. Yet, in Jesus Christ, conflict among peoples is ended. We lay down our guns. We recognize what God has known ever since Eve and Adam. We are brother and sister. Let the reunion begin. And let it begin in the church.

CHAPTER 6

Preaching on the Restoration of Women

For the past thirty years, the contemporary church has been involved in a discussion regarding the place of women in the church. The spectrum of opinion runs from one pole, at which people think that women should be subject to men, to the opposite pole, at which people think that women can participate fully in all aspects of Christian community. Luke offers a contribution to this conversation.

In this chapter I first review basic aspects in views of women in the First Testament, Judaism, and the wider Greco-Roman world. The core of the chapter traces the Lukan author's picture of the restoration of women in the reign of God. After a brief statement of the contemporary importance of Luke's perspective, I end with a sermon on this theme.

Women in Judaism and in Wider Hellenistic Settings

The motif of the end times' being similar to the beginning times is important with respect to the restoration of women in the realm of God. According to Genesis 1:26–27, women and men each bear the image of God. Women and men are to exercise dominion in their limited spheres in the same way that God exercises dominion in the cosmic sphere. To exercise dominion is not to exercise power arbitrarily, but to help all created entities live in relationships of encouragement and support. Women and men share this responsibility equally. Genesis 1–2 contains no suggestion of hierarchy.

Women become subordinate to men only after the first couple eat the forbidden fruit (Gen. 3:1–13). God cursed the whole world (3:14–19). The portion of the curse directed against women includes becoming subordinate to men (3:16).

Henceforth, women and men typically exist in a patriarchal relationship in which males have authority over women in many arenas of life. Women in Israel were typically under the care of a male. A woman's primary roles included childbearing and tending to the needs of her husband and children. Women received little education and did not participate widely in public life. Women seldom owned property. Women had some legal rights, but the legal system favored males. Women participated in public religious life in limited ways (they could not, for instance, serve as priests). On the positive side, women were not supposed to be treated as chattel. Men were enjoined to care for women.

Within such limitations, Proverbs 31:10–31 pictures the ideal woman of the period as vested with decision-making power and as a creative thinker and actor. Furthermore, the First Testament pictures women and situations that critique and transcend patriarchy (e.g., Miriam and Deborah are described as prophets; Ruth acts as a self–determining agent). However, hierarchicalism is the usual pattern of relationship.

Preachers often quote statements like the following as if they comprehensively represent attitudes toward women in Judaism in the Hellenistic age. "Happy is he whose children are males, and woe to him whose children are females."[1] "Whoever teaches his daughter the torah teaches her obscenity."[2]

While such citations illustrate a strand of thinking in Judaism, they are not altogether representative. Marcus Barth, a noted scholar of this period, notes a cultural trend "toward the emancipation of women" in the Hellenistic age.[3] In many sectors women could own property, run businesses, and live by themselves. Luke–Acts contain illustrations of women in each of these categories. Education was available to some women. A few women founded their own religions.

The trend toward liberation took place in Judaism as well. In this vein, to the surprise of many Christians, Jacob Neusner, a leading authority on Judaism in antiquity, titled a recent book

How the Rabbis Liberated Women. Neusner finds that much rabbinic literature (written slightly after the Second Testament) articulates values that accord women

> the standing and powers of sentient beings, possessed of a role that was, if not entirely equal, then corresponding to that of men in critical transactions in their existence. [The rabbis] made [women] active, responsible beings; they legislated to take account of their intentionality. Women were not only chattel, talking cows, animate sofas as some have maintained.[4]

Indeed, there is considerable evidence that women could even serve as leaders of synagogues.[5]

The changes for women were sufficiently far-reaching and unsettling that some people in the Hellenistic era sought to restrict the level of women's freedom and even to return to some of the earlier limitations on women. Hence, communities in the Hellenistic age were conflicted over how to prescribe the role of women. Scholars are divided as to the degree to which the writings of the Lukan author support emancipation and the degree to which these texts react against the movement toward self-determination for women. I think that Luke leans toward the former because the reinstitution of egalitarian relationships between women and men is part of the eschatological manifestation of the rule of God.

Impulses toward Restoration of Women in Luke–Acts

When the reign of God is fully manifest, relationships between women and men will be altogether restored. Jesus and the Christian community embody aspects of this restoration.[6] Indeed, in Luke–Acts, women sometimes model how to respond to the divine rule and serve as its agents. However, while Jesus and the early church point toward the restoration, they do not fully reclaim the world of Eden. Women are not included among the twelve apostles. Women appear infrequently in Acts, and they are seldom cast in roles that transcend the usual roles of women in antiquity. These books contain an *impulse* toward restoration that will be completed when the new age is fully manifest.

Impulses toward Restoration in Luke

The theme of impulse toward the restoration of women is established at the very beginning of Luke. The male figures are relatively unresponsive to the heavenly messages announcing the manifestation of the divine rule, whereas the women immediately recognize the significance of these events and respond accordingly. Although an angel announces the birth of John to Zechariah, the old priest is disbelieving and is struck mute (Lk. 1:8–23). By contrast, Elizabeth welcomes the news (2:24–25). Zechariah's speech returns only after the priest accepts his spouse's instruction (1:59–66).

Scholars often speak of Mary as the model believer (1:26–38). She is a vulnerable young woman to whom the angel Gabriel comes with the surprising news that she will be an integral part of the regeneration of the world by giving birth to Jesus. Without consulting a male, she accepts this divine initiative. Mary is the first preacher to announce the significance of Jesus' ministry (1:46–55).

Introducing a motif that recurs several times in Luke–Acts, a woman and a man jointly interpret the manifestation of the reign of God through Jesus. Both Simeon and Anna are prophets (2:25–38). When both prophesy, the listener subtly hears echoes of the shared leadership of the first couple in Eden.

Jesus uses the healing of a woman as a prime illustration in his inaugural sermon at Nazareth (4:25–26). Jesus performs other miracles in behalf of women. He raises the widow's only son at Nain. The death of the only son placed the woman in economic and social peril; the raising from the dead provides for her economic and social well-being (7:11–17). Jesus forgives a woman who is a sinner (7:36–50). The content of the woman's sin is not named, but the term sinner resonates with the profound negativity described in the previous chapter. Jesus describes this woman's faith and behavior as a model (7:44–50).

In 8:1–3 Luke reports that a group of women helped finance the mission of Jesus with their own money. These women do not depend on men for economic resources. The women are means of God's provision for Jesus and the disciples (cf. Lk. 12:22–34).

A woman who is religiously unclean because of a hemorrhage makes her way to Jesus. The healing both restores her physical health and returns her to the community (8:42–48). That she is a model for Luke's listeners is dramatically indicated by the insertion of her story into the larger story of the raising of Jairus' daughter (8:40–42, 49–54). The woman exemplifies the faith that is possible for Jairus and his family. When Jesus raises the daughter, the listener realizes that we, too, can live in such faith.

Jesus visits the home of Mary and Martha, who live independently (10:38–42). Mary partakes of Jesus' rabbinical instruction. Martha engages in the traditional woman's role of preparing and serving a meal. However, Jesus sanctions Mary's behavior, thus indicating that women have full access to instruction in discipleship.

Jesus straightens a bent-over women and calls her "daughter of Abraham" (13:10–17). This title indicates that Jesus regards her as a full member of the covenantal community. Furthermore, Jesus defends against opposition the healing of the woman on the Sabbath.

Jesus laments the coming destruction of Jerusalem with a feminine image. "How often have I desired to gather your children together as a hen gathers her brood under her wings, and you were not willing" (13:31–34). This image evokes an aspect of Jewish tradition that compared God to a woman (e.g., Deut. 32:18; Ps. 22:9–10; Prov. 1:20–33; Isa. 42:14; 46:3–4; 49:15; 66:7–16; Jer. 31:15–22; Hos. 11:1–11). Such imagery reminds hearers that women bear the image of God and that the experience of women can teach the community aspects of the divine nature and activity.

We see the motif of joint representation of women and men when Jesus tells the twin parables of the shepherd who finds the lost sheep and the woman who finds the lost coin (Lk. 15:3–10). The latter parable compares God to a woman (cf. 13:31–34).

In the midst of a discourse on the coming of the realm of God, Jesus tells the parable of the widow and the unjust judge (18:1–8). The parable is an argument from the lesser to the greater. If an unjust judge eventually gives justice to a persistent widow, how much more will God manifest the divine rule for a broken world? Jesus uses the behavior of a woman as an example for the church to persist in prayer in the way that the woman persisted in pressing her case. Furthermore, the woman models protest against injustice.

Some Sadducces tell Jesus about a woman whose husband dies. According to custom, she then becomes the wife of his brother. That brother and his other brothers die, so that she is married in serial fashion to seven different men. The Sadduccees ask, "In the resurrection, therefore, whose wife will the woman be?" Jesus points out that the woman will be liberated from such confusion of relationship in the resurrection. For the resurrected ones "neither marry nor are given in marriage" (20:27–38).

Most interpreters take the story of the poor widow putting two copper coins into the temple treasury as a model of generosity (21:1–4). That interpretation is plausible given the Lukan author's interest in encouraging members of the community to provide materially for one another. However, an alternative reading regards the text as a criticism of the treasury that exploited the widow of "*all* that she had to live on." The narrative is an implicit call for religious systems to act on behalf of justice. Such systems are not to be unjust.[7]

Women follow Jesus to the cross. When they beat their breasts and wail, Jesus speaks to them as "Daughters of Jerusalem," that is, as representatives of the covenantal community to whom God's victory is promised (Lk. 23:26–31; Zeph. 3:14; Zech. 9:9). When Jesus is crucified the women faithfully remain with him (Lk. 23:48–49). Women see that Jesus' body is anointed for a proper Jewish burial (23:54–55). Even in the face of Jesus' death, the women are obedient to the commandment to rest on the Sabbath (23:56).

On the first day of the week, some women are preparing to anoint the body when they discover that Jesus' tomb is empty. They demonstrate that they understand the heart of Jesus' teaching concerning the manifestation of the new world when they immediately recognize the significance of the resurrection and become the first Christian preachers by telling the apostles what had happened. By contrast, the apostles did not initially believe the women (24:1–11). Luke underscores the veracity of the women (24:22–24).

However, the Lukan author does not have a myopic view of women. Like Lot's wife, women can be unfaithful and can be condemned (17:22–37, especially 32, 34–35).

Women in the Community of the Restoration in Acts

In Acts, women are integrated into the community of the restoration from its earliest days. The women in Acts do not play roles that are as frequent or prominent as those of the apostles and many other community leaders. Nonetheless, the impetus toward restoration is pronounced.

As Acts opens, Judas' death has reduced the number of apostles from twelve to eleven. The author portrays women as a part of the community of prayer that undergirds the selection of Matthias to take Judas' place among the Twelve (Acts 1:12–14).

On Pentecost, Peter draws from Joel 2:28–32 to indicate that the Spirit is being poured out on sons *and* daughters who shall prophesy, and on male *and* female slaves. The Spirit enables women to function fully in Christian community. The mention of women and men recalls Eve and Adam jointly exercising dominion in Eden. In a summary of the evangelistic success of the church, the author points out that both men and women were added to the church in large numbers (5:14).

Some Greek-speaking Jewish believers (Hellenists) complain that the Aramaic-speaking Christians ("the Hebrews") were not giving the Greek-speaking widows a fair allotment of the daily distribution of food. Enacting an aspect of the parable of the widow and the unjust judge (Lk. 18:1–8), the community provides justice for the Greeks by instituting the office of deacon (Acts 6:1–6). Faithful witnesses in Acts are frequently persecuted. Women are among them (e.g., Acts 8:3; 9:2; 22:4).

The ministry of Jesus in Luke patterns the ministry of the church in Acts. Peter embodies the realm of God by raising Tabitha (Dorcas) from the dead (Acts 9:36–41; cf. Lk. 7:11–17). Such stories establish continuity between the actions of God in the First Testament and the church (e.g., 1 Kings 17:17–24; 2 Kings 4:18–37).

Peter was imprisoned and guarded by four squads of soldiers (a huge number). In the night, in an event reminiscent of both the exodus from Egypt and the release of Jesus from the tomb, Peter was freed from prison. Peter went to the house of Mary where "many were praying." Mary was a leader in the early Christian community. When Peter arrived, Rhoda the maid answered the door. Like the women at the empty tomb who became the first to announce the resurrection, Rhoda announced to the others in the house that Peter was at the gate. However, like the apostles responding to the women who came from the tomb, the people in the house did not initially believe Rhoda (Acts 12:12–17; cf. Lk. 24:1–11). The listener, however, is encouraged (again) to recognize the truthfulness of the testimony of a woman.

The author gently reminds the reader that Judaism is matrilineal (Acts 16:1). At Philippi, Paul and Silas preach to women who gather at a place of prayer. Lydia, a seller of purple cloth (and mentioned without connection to a male) is among them. The text assumes that Lydia was proprietress of her own business. Her conversion signals that independent women of means are to be welcomed into the Christian community (Acts 16:11–15; cf. my comments below on Acts 13:50; 17:4, 12, 34).

The next narrative reminds auditors that the Christian community is trans–social-class. Paul exorcises a slave woman. The exorcism incurs the wrath of the owners of the woman and leads to the imprisonment of Paul and Silas. Like Jesus, the disciples face confrontation in order to liberate women from Satan (Acts 16:16–40; cf. Lk. 13:10–17).

The author of the book stresses repeatedly that women respond positively to the news of the fresh manifestation of the reign of God in Thessalonica, Berea, and Athens. The respondents include women of high standing (Acts 17:4, 12, 34). The mention of women of high standing is a direct foil to the author's earlier note that some women of high standing opposed the news of the regeneration (Acts 13:50; cf. Acts 16:11–15 above). These references remind the community that such women can have a place in the Christian community and that high standing is not, in itself, a credential for admission or reason for rejection.

The author's treatment of women and men in partnership in the community reaches a high point in the story of Priscilla and Aquila. Paul stays with them. When the learned Alexandrian Apollos arrives, Priscilla joins her spouse Aquila in teaching Apollos (Acts 18:1–4, 24–28). It would be anachronistic to claim that Priscilla and Aquila were the first clergy couple, but the author portrays them as partners in the ministry of teaching.

In a direct echo of Acts 2:17–18, Paul encounters four women who prophesy (Acts 21:7–9). This passage prompts the hearer to listen for women who are prophesying in the church subsequent to the close of the narrative of Acts.

However, the author's picture of women in Acts is not completely positive. Women can engage in destructive behavior. For example, Sapphira joins Ananias in lying to the Holy Spirit and is struck dead. (Acts 5:1–11). Other women also obstruct the witness (e.g., 13:50). A riot breaks out among Gentiles who worship the goddess Artemis (19:23–41); women, like men, can provide inspiration for idolatry. Drusilla, Jewish spouse of Felix, remains silent when Paul discusses "justice, self-control, and the coming judgment," with the result that Paul's imprisonment is prolonged (24:24–26). Agrippa and his spouse, Bernice, hear Paul's testimony and conclude (in a manner similar to Pilate's conclusion about Jesus), "This man is doing nothing to deserve death or imprisonment." While the couple lament Paul's situation, they take no steps to set the record straight (25:13–26:32, especially 30–32; cf. Lk. 23:13–16).

The Restoration of Women in the Church Today

The writing of Luke–Acts may not articulate a picture of women fully restored. However, it pulses in that direction and, hence, calls the contemporary Christian community to reclaim roles and relationships of women for the fullness of divine purposes. To adapt a phrase from Robin Scroggs, Luke–Acts moves toward "eschatological women," that is, women who live in the present as if the restoration is fully accomplished.[8] In the eschatological community, women and men are joined as egalitarian partners as they were in Eden.

While the Lukan author's portrayal of the experience of women presupposes a tendency toward emancipation already underway, he also reminds us to name circumstances in the church and world today that continue the curse of Genesis upon women (and upon the relationships of women and men). For instance, in many Christian communities, women encounter a "stained glass ceiling," that is, a point in leadership in the church beyond which they cannot progress.[9] Many congregations and judicatories have invisible barriers that prohibit women from serving congregations of a certain size (usually large ones) or serving as certain kinds of judicatory officials. How does the fuller manifestation of the reign of God critique the restricted life of women in the old age? How should the life of the eschatological woman take form in today's church and world?

The Lukan author emphasizes that God is graciously active in the experience of women in restoration. The preacher can ask, "How is God similarly present in the experience of *women* today?" I italicize the term *women* to emphasize two things. First, women's experience is a source for theological reflection and, indeed, revelation. Second, many sermons dwell disproportionately on male experience, use illustrations from male spheres, assume male practices, and use male norms to gauge things that are more and less valued. Historically the church has given little attention to women's experience either as a source for theological reflection or for discussion directly in the sermon.

In Luke–Acts, women frequently have clear visions of God's purposes of restoration. The preacher can help the congregation listen to contemporary women who similarly have insight into the divine presence and activity. Who, for instance, functions for us in the way the widow functions in the parable of the widow and the unjust judge?

The author of Luke–Acts emphasizes that women often model healthy responses to the awareness of God's grace. The preacher can turn to Mary and other women as models for the congregation of how we can respond to divine initiatives for renewal. The sermon can make use of strong images of contemporary women who are models of faithfulness.

Scholars note that the Lukan author frequently pairs female and male persons or images. This motif climaxes with the depiction of Priscilla and Aquila as joint teachers of Apollos. This theme can lead the preacher to reflect directly on ways in which women and men can embody the restored community of leadership in the church (and in the wider world) by serving in partnership with one another.

I have heard Christians say that the church is simply being politically correct when seeking women for positions of leadership and when advocating justice for women. The preacher needs to help congregations understand that such concerns are not merely matters of political correctness. From Luke's perspective, the church's efforts in these regards are rooted in the divine activity to restore this broken world.

A Sermon on the Theme of the Restoration of Women

When I lead Bible studies in local congregations, people often ask for information about the seminary at which I teach. I report that our seminary, like many others, enrolls more than 50 percent women in the degree program for ministerial ordination.

This report elicits responses like these: "I am so excited. The church is finally awakening to the creativity of women." Applause. "Well...I don't know about this turn of events. Doesn't the Bible say that women are the weaker sex and that they should keep silent in the church?" A few nods of agreement. "Well, I'll be darned. I guess we'll have a woman preacher one of these days."

After such a session, an older woman often catches me in the kitchen and says something like, "I had a good life as an English teacher. But in the back of my mind, I felt called to be a minister. But at that time, it just didn't seem possible." Can you feel the poignancy?

The world has not always wrestled with such questions. In Eden, Adam and Eve were partners in managing the garden. That's part of what the Bible means when it says, "So God created humankind in [the divine] image…male and female [God] created them" (Gen. 1:27). Women and men both bear the image of God and are both given dominion. The image of God and exercising dominion add up to the capacity to do in our small worlds what God does in the world at large: to help all things relate to one another as God intends in mutuality and support. The woman and the man relate to one another in the way that God wants all creatures to relate. The woman and the man are partners in helping the world become one great community.

So why aren't things still that way? The report for women is mixed today. Yes, there are many opportunities for women that were not so available even a few years ago. For example, there is employment that was previously restricted almost altogether to men, opportunities to rise in management, laws to prohibit discrimination based on gender.

Yet many women today live east of Eden, so to speak. A disproportionate number of women live in poverty. Many towns have shelters for battered women. A remarkable new book chronicles the pain of women who have felt silenced by the culture and the church. They have not felt allowed to speak. This enforced silence seems a prison.[10]

Frequently, I encounter women who have graduated from our seminary and been ordained. They start their first ministries on high notes. But when I later encounter them, things have changed. Figuratively speaking, men have beaten them up. Other women resist their ministry. One woman who had been ordained just a few months said, "I wonder if I want to continue." Four years of college. Four years of seminary. Educational debt in excess of $50,000. Six months in the ministry. "I wonder if I want to continue."

The Bible explains the change from Eden to east of Eden mythologically with the story of the fall. Adam and Eve ate of the forbidden fruit. When they did, sin entered the world and infected all relationships. Genesis succinctly states two of the most dramatic things to befall women. "In pain you shall bring forth children, yet your desire shall be for your husband, and he shall rule over you" (Gen. 3:16). Pain in childbearing. Subordination. Only after the fall are women subordinate to men. Secondary status was not God's original plan.

Subsequently, in the world of the First Testament, women typically lived restricted lives. They had to be attached to a man. They mostly stayed home, cooked, raised children, tended the men, and helped around the place. Men were supposed to treat women with respect, but men clearly had the upper hand.

By the time of Jesus things were loosening for women. In many sectors women could own their own property, run their own businesses, and live by themselves. Yet, welcome as these improvements were, they were incomplete. The Jewish people never forgot Eden. In fact, many Jewish people believed that, in order to be just, God would restore the world to be similar to Eden.

From the very beginning of Luke, the author signals us that this restoration is underway for women and for relationships between women and men.

- An angel tells Elizabeth and Zechariah that they are going to give birth to John the Baptist. Zechariah does not believe and is struck mute. Elizabeth believes. Zechariah does not speak again until Elizabeth properly instructs him.

- Scholars refer to Mary as the model believer. When she recognizes God's grace she immediately responds in trust, "Let it be with me according to your word."

- At his first sermon in Nazareth, Jesus uses an illustration to show that women would be a part of the divine restoration of the world.

- Jesus raises the son of a widow in Nain and heals women.

- Jesus calls a woman "Daughter of Abraham," indicating that she is a full member of the covenantal community.

- Women bankroll the ministry of Jesus and the apostles.

- God is compared to a woman who searches all night for a lost coin.

- When Jesus is crucified, women remain loyal to him to the agonizing end and beyond. They return to the tomb to anoint the body in the proper Jewish way.

- Women–yes, women–are the first to announce the news of the resurrection. What is this act? Nothing less than the first Christian preaching.

- In the congregation in which I grew up, the whole congregation held its breath when women were first elected to the governing body. That was in the late 1960s. We have been only two millennia catching up to the early church that had women present at the very first business meeting to elect Matthias as successor to Judas.
- Peter quotes the prophet Joel: The Holy Spirit will be poured on women and men. Both will prophesy.
- Dorcas is raised from the dead.
- Lydia, seller of expensive purple cloth, joins the community of the restoration. The missionaries honor the depth of her faith by staying with her.
- Rhoda carries the news that Peter is released from prison.
- Priscilla is joint teacher with Aquila for the classically trained Apollos.
- The daughters of Philip are prophets.

Now, to be honest, there are not as many women in this roll call as I would like. I wish women were included among the Twelve. I wish that women played a more prominent role in the leadership of the early church. But...But...But...The impulse is still unmistakable. God is moving to restore the world of women. And God is moving to restore the world through the restoration of women.

Truth to tell, it doesn't always seem that way to women today. In poverty. Battered in the home. Beat up in the church. That's why we need Luke and Acts.

This story reminds us of what God wants for women. And of the fact that God is at work for women. Luke's narrative critiques the efforts of both men and women to restrict the roles of women in the church and in the wider world.

This story reminds women and men that partnership in tending the garden of life is our original vocation. God, through the Holy Spirit, makes it possible for our churches and communities to become full partners with women in the quest for a world that is itself a community of partners in serving in God's love and justice for all.

Teaching in a theological seminary, I see this restoration at work all the time. Women who are uncertain and tenative enroll in our classes. They are aware that that they are on a journey, but they do not know quite where it will lead. Some who have been denied and battered show up in our classes. And before our very eyes, renewal takes place as they discover their possibilities in God's new world.

Sometimes the restoration sneaks up on you. My spouse is ordained. In 1977 we began serving as co-pastors of First Christian Church (Disciples of Christ) in Grand Island, Nebraska. We were not the first clergy couple in our denomination, or even in Grand Island, but we still felt a little bit like pioneers in this form of partnership. After we had been in Grand Island for a while, we were with a group of older women, talking informally about how my spouse and I were dividing responsibilities. One of the older women, who had grown up in a sod house, commented that such a shared life was nothing new to her husband and her. "In the Depression, we didn't have gas for the tractor. We worked alongside each other in the field, driving the horses together. I could work as long as he could any day. And he learned how to change a diaper too." Pause. Wink. "What you're doing ain't so different to this generation."

The book that I mentioned a few minutes ago is titled *Saved from Silence.* For women who have been silenced, the power to *speak* is itself restorative.

There is another chapter in the story of the young woman I mentioned earlier, the one who went to school eight years to prepare for ministry, racked up $50,000 in educational debts, and after six months said, "I wonder if I want to continue." When some of the women in the congregation heard that their pastor was discouraged, they began to meet as a prayer and support group and to identify ways they could try to change the congregational system that diminished their minister's service. Over the next couple of years, things did begin to change, and today that congregation lives a lot less east of Eden. Perfect? No. A better network of partnership in ministry? Yes.

Of course, restoration will not be complete until the realm of God is fully manifested. Until then, we can expect difficulty, resistance, and even conflict. And we will have to experiment to determine the optimum ways that restored relationships can take place in our time. Sometimes we need to say some hard things to one another about the ways in which we repress women and our need to repent.

Nonetheless, through such processes God is at work to re-create relationships among women and men as a great community of partnership. God promises the gift of the Holy Spirit to strengthen all who participate in this movement. I want to do all that I can to help the church become a community of the restoration. I hope you will too.

CHAPTER 7

Preaching on Poverty, Abundance, and the Use of Material Resources

Expositors almost always call attention to poverty, abundance, and the relationship of the community to material resources as central concerns of Luke and Acts. This theme is important in literary and theological analysis of Luke's writings. In addition, contemporary phenomena press this material on our consciousness with urgency. Poverty is increasing in our world. Disparity grows between the poor and the wealthy. The Christian community is confused. Should we spend money on institutional maintenance and new buildings when people are hungry and homeless?

Luke's perspectives on poverty, abundance, and the use of material resources are quite provocative in our context. This chapter first reviews the relationship among material resources, poverty, and abundance in the First Testament and Judaism. I then interpret the understanding of this theme in Luke–Acts. A few comments on the importance of these materials for the Christian community today precede a sermon on the theme.

Material Resources, Poverty, and Abundance in Jewish Tradition

The story of creation is foundational to the stream of Jewish thinking that feeds the Lukan author's perception of the relationship among material resources, poverty, and abundance.

God created the world as a material realm. God created people as material beings. The human being is an integrated whole in whom mind, emotions, and actions are inseparably interconnected. This worldview does not divide self or universe into realms of (a) the essential and good nonmaterial dimension (spirit) and (b) the nonessential and sometimes evil material dimension (flesh, body). The things that happen in our material selves and in our material communities are things that happen to the essential us. The author of Luke–Acts assumes this material view of self and world.

The story of creation reveals divine intention for the world: to be a place of genuine community of mutual support (Gen. 1:1–2:25). The world is to be a community that provides abundantly for all creatures so that every creature can "be all that they can be" (to borrow a slogan from the U.S. Army). The Lukan author recollects this ideal world as a paradigm for the renewed world.

However, through the misuse of material resources (eating the forbidden fruit), the fall interrupts this scenario (Gen. 3:1–2, especially 14–19). After the fall, the human relationship with material things is enigmatic. While materiality is still a means of blessing, the misuse of materiality can now curse. The world of nature is disrupted.

Poverty and excessive wealth come into being only after the fall. Each represents a distortion of divine intention. On one hand, lack of adequate material resources in human life (and in the natural world) goes against the purposes of God. It causes community members to become absorbed with survival and to be unable to participate fully in community. On the other hand, people distort the purpose of God when they have enough material resources to be secure, but accumulate an overabundance. Indeed, acquisition can become idolatrous. Material things are not ends in themselves, but means through which the purpose of God can be embodied.

Even in the post-fall world, God wants all in the human family to enjoy material security. This hope is included in the call to Sarah and Abraham that through them "all the families of the earth shall be blessed" (Gen. 12:3). Israel's communal life is to demonstrate how provision can be made for all in the human family.

At the most obvious level, the Jewish communities develop laws and strategies that provide for people whose capacity to enjoy fullness of community and to contribute to it is threatened by insecurity. They are represented by the poor, orphans, widows, strangers, and others whose lives are threatened by lack of material resources (e.g., Ex. 22:21–17; Lev. 25:8–55, especially 8–24; Deut. 15:1–18, especially 7–11). Members of the community become instruments of divine providence by sharing their goods. Offerings through the tabernacle, temple, and synagogue provide social structure to collect and disseminate such resources. At a less obvious level, this motif is pastoral guidance for those who have abundance not to become idolatrous of wealth. Sharing should help them remember that all material things originate in God, who intends them for the blessing of all in community. The act of sharing should help those who have abundance remember that the covenant with God is simultaneously covenant with the community.

The classical prophets call attention to injustices in Israel's common life (e.g., Isa.1:12–17; Jer. 22:13–17; Am. 2:4–8). Some people neglect and exploit the poor. God condemns this behavior. Indeed, a community's care of the poor is an index of its faithfulness to (or violation of) covenant. It contributes to community collapse. These prophets plead for the community to restructure its social operations to make abundance available for all (e.g., Isa. 56:8–9; Am. 5:21–24).

The attitude that the community is a means of material blessing to all characterizes Judaism in the Hellenistic age. Tobit speaks for much of this literature, "Give alms from your possessions, and do not let our eye begrudge the gift when you make it. Do not turn your face away from anyone who is poor, and the face of God will not be turned away from you" (Tob. 4:7–8; cf. Sir. 4:1–10).

Several apocalyptic authors presume that in the realm of God, all people will enjoy abundance (e.g., *Testament of Judah* 25:4; *Sibylline Oracle* 3:378; 8:208). There will be neither poverty nor unneeded wealth. Some writers envision a time when the poor will be exalted over the rich (e.g., *2 Baruch* 70:4) While waiting for the apocalypse, the community is to tend to the poor (e.g., 2 Esd. 14:13). However, God will condemn those who have neglected or exploited the poor (*1 Enoch* 94:7–8; 96:4–8; 97:8–10).

The Qumran community, believing that they were living in the last days, rejected private ownership. When people became full members of the community, they turned their property over to the community (*1QS* 6:19, 22, 25; 10:19). All in the community lived on the basis of the accumulated goods. The Qumran community believed that the eschatological world would be structured so that all lived out of a common and abundant supply. Other Jewish people regarded such sharing of material possessions as an ideal.[1]

Common ownership was part of the social vision of many philosophies and religions in the Mediterranean world.[2] Pythagoras, for instance, lived communally with his followers. Plato regarded private property as a root of evil since it created conditions for selfishness. The Cynics believed that the divine force created all things for the common good. The Stoics considered the model community one in which all things belonged to all people and in which people worked together for the common good. Neo-Pythagoreans reclaimed Pythagoras' idea of all living together so that no one would have need.

The Lukan author draws inspiration from the Jewish anticipation of communal abundance in the new world while modifying it somewhat. In addition, Luke's vision is obviously sympathetic to the ideal of common ownership found in the wider Hellenistic world.

Luke–Acts: Sharing Material Resources as Means to Community Blessing

The themes of poverty, abundance, and relationship with material resources in Luke–Acts develop along the lines just sketched. These documents anticipate the realm of God as a world of abundance for all. In the meantime, the community is a means whereby God provides for the poor while helping to free the rich from greed. Jesus both teaches this dimension of the reign of God and embodies aspects of it. The early church anticipates aspects of the abundant eschatological communality.

In one respect the interpreter must exercise care. When heard in isolation from the larger corpus of Luke–Acts, several statements in Luke seem to imply that the realm of God will contain a simple reversal in the present situation of the poor and the rich, as if the poor will become rich and the rich will become poor. When read in the light of the larger narrative, we realize that these themes serve a pastoral function as warning, a call to repent, and an exhortation to use material resources faithfully. As Luke Timothy Johnson (a major scholar of the Second Testament at Emory University) pointed out long ago, the use of possessions both provides (or denies) material help *and* functions as a vital symbol of deeper understandings of life and relationship.[3] Sharing (or not sharing) materially with other people expresses one's relationship with the community.

Mary reminds listeners that God has proven faithful to the poor in the past, and that God has dethroned the unfaithful rich (Lk. 1:53–55). The listener thus understands that the Lukan author's presentation of this theme is continuous with Judaism and is trustworthy.

John the Baptist calls listeners to repent of their false attachment to material resources and to share their possessions with the needy (Lk. 3:10–14). All who repent in this way are welcome in the community of the new age.

In his inaugural sermon at Nazareth, Jesus borrows Isaiah's description of the eschatological age to indicate that the forces of this age are now being manifested through the ministry of Jesus (Lk. 4:18–19). This age contains "good news to the poor," that is, a time of abundance. Luke–Acts narrates ways that God is proleptically demonstrating this abundance. For instance, Peter, James, and John fish all night but catch nothing. Jesus speaks. They catch so many fish that their nets break (5:1–10). They are so confident of this providence that they leave everything and follow Jesus (cf. 5:27–28). Through Jesus, God feeds five thousand people in the wilderness (9:10–17).

Lukan Beatitudes assert that the poor and the hungry are blessed because they will be a part of the realm of God and will be filled. By contrast, the rich and the full are cursed ("Woe") because they have already received consolation and are full now (6:20–21, 24–25). In this context, to be blessed is to be included in the apocalyptic realm of God; for them, the end time will be like the beginning time. To receive woe is to fall under the apocalyptic judgment. Furthermore, we should multivalently understand poor, hungry, rich, and full. At a basic level, these categories include the economically destitute and wealthy. In addition, some of Jesus' followers fall into these categories, for example, the Twelve have given up everything (i.e., have become poor, Lk. 5:1–10, 27–28; 9:1–6, 57–61; 18:28–30) and become hungry (with the crowd in the wilderness, 9:10–17). The members of the early church divest themselves of their possessions (Acts 2:44–47; 4:32–39). This passage assures them that they will be a part of the new era of unending abundance (cf. Lk. 18:28–30).

Many wealthy folk turn away from the opportunity to be a part of the realm of God (e.g., Lk. 12:13–21; 18:18–27). However, through repentance and sharing, the wealthy in this life can become a part of the community witnessing to the new world (e.g., Lk. 19:1–10).

A group of women financially support Jesus and his entourage, thus demonstrating that sharing through community is a means whereby God provides for those in need in this age (Lk. 8:1–3). Their act is a prototype of God's care for the poor in Acts.

My colleague J. Gerald Janzen points out that the prayer that Jesus teaches his disciples is a chiasm whose central concern is bread (Lk. 11:2–4).

A Hallowed be your name

  B Your [realm] come

    C Give us each day our daily bread

  B' And forgive us our sins, etc.

A' And do not bring us to the time of trial.

In antiquity, bread was a staple food, especially for the poor. In Luke–Acts, bread is another multivalent symbol, not only of provision for day-to-day existence but also of the abundance of the eschatological age. The parable of the friend at midnight and subsequent teachings reinforce this point: God provides for all who witness to that realm (Lk. 11:5–13). This provision includes the awareness of the Holy Spirit, an agent of God who empowers the manifestation of the divine realm. Daily bread prefigures the unending supply of the eschatological age. The breaking of the bread in the community is particularly symbolic of such provision (cf. Lk. 22:19; 24:30–35; Acts 2:42–46; 20:7–11; 27:35).

The parable of the barn-building fool, a warning to greedy people and an implicit reminder that material resources are not for self-indulgence (Lk. 12:13–21), introduces a sustained discussion on the relationship of disciples and material resources. Jesus' disciples need not worry about building larger and larger barns because God creates structures to mediate providence for the community (Lk. 12:22–34). God cares for those who seek the divine realm, just as God cares for the ravens and clothes the lilies. The security of the knowledge that God provides for Jesus' followers frees them to sell their possessions and give alms, that is, to use material resources for building the community. The outcome of this teaching for a church living in the time of transition between the old age and the new is revealed in Acts 2:42–47 and 4:32–39.

As previously noted, the apocalyptic tradition anticipates a great banquet to celebrate the day when the realm of God is fully operative throughout the cosmos. In addition, eating has special significance to the poor. In this old world they struggle each day for food. God's new world will provide for them abundantly. This symbolism is nearly always present in the Lukan author's references to meals, for example, 14:12–24. The parable of the great banquet explicitly uses such a meal as an image for the realm of God (14:15). God is inviting people to come to the banquet, that is, to participate in the divine realm, but many refuse because of their attachments to the old world. While these refusals make it impossible for the refusers to be a part of the celebration, they do not prevent the banquet from continuing. God brings the poor, crippled, blind, and lame (14:16–24). The life of the Christian community becomes such a banquet when it joins such people in a banquet of food and resources for all. A banquet, of course, involves the actual feeding of people.

The parable of the rich person and Lazarus vividly encapsulates Luke's understanding of the relationship among poverty, wealth, material resources, and the reign of God (16:19–31). Listeners feel the injustice of the suffering of Lazarus, especially when the rich person has command of resources that could immediately relieve Lazarus' condition. The parable poignantly paints their reversal of fortune in the age to come. Luke's pastoral point is expressed in 16:27–31. Luke's church knows Moses and the prophets as well as the one who is risen from the dead. Therefore, these listeners can avoid the fate of the rich person by repenting and sharing their resources.

The rich ruler is a similar negative example. The ruler wants to inherit eternal life (i.e., to be a part of the great restoration) but is unwilling to sell everything, distribute the money to the poor, and follow Jesus (18:18–25). While this requirement makes it very hard for people to be saved, Jesus replies that "what is impossible for mortals is possible for God," that is, God is creating conditions in which people feel so secure that they can give up the security created by old-age behaviors and can trust in the security of God's realm (18:26–30).

This turn of events takes place at the home of Zacchaeus, a chief tax collector who is rich and a sinner (19:1–10). However, unlike the rich person in 16:19–31 and the rich ruler of 18:18–25, Zacchaeus immediately repents, gives half of his earthly possessions to the poor, and makes restitution four times over to those he has defrauded. "Today," Jesus says, "salvation [i.e., welcome into the divine realm] has come to this house." The listener, too, can receive this benediction by acting as Zacchaeus does.

In the parable of the pounds, the situation of the church, waiting for the apocalypse, is compared to the situation of the slaves while a noble person is away. The parable admonishes the community to witness to the realm of God with the energy of the first two slaves and to avoid the fate of the third (19:11–27). While the parable is not an allegory, the fact that the pounds are material resources prompts us to ponder whether we are making enough use of our spectrum of resources to witness to the great regeneration.

As noted above, most interpreters take the widow's offering as an example to be emulated (21:1–4). However, we can also hear the story as a critique of religious institutions that ask people to give up their means of life to support the institution.

While Acts does not contain as much material regarding material possessions, the attitude toward possessions in this part of the story is revealed in two key texts (Acts 2:44–47; 4:32–37). In the Lukan author's idealized memory, the early Christian community both provided material blessing for the poor and gave the wealthy opportunity to free themselves from the idolatry of wealth. "All who believed were together and had all things in common; they would sell their possessions and goods and distribute the proceeds to all, as any had need" (Acts 2:44–45). The community treasury provided for the poor. Putting one's goods in the hands of the community relieves the problems of greed and idolatry. Sharing of material resources embodies the bond of the community.

Scholars are divided about whether community members sold their goods and placed the proceeds in the common treasury of the community of witness or whether they retained individual ownership and sold possessions as need arose in the community. I tend toward the former interpretation because private ownership was not a part of life in the garden and because the ideal of communal living was widely known in Judaism. Furthermore, living out of a common treasury would more fully embody the new world than retaining individual property rights. However, either interpretation comes to the same end: the day-to-day life of the community both provides for the practical needs of the saints and demonstrates the attractiveness of life in the new age. Listeners should be motivated to take steps of repentance and sharing to be a part of the new world.

The narrative of Ananias and Sapphira is a reverse image of the sharing characteristic of the incipient community (Acts 5:1–11). This story is a warning: People who hoard their own goods and who do not put their resources in the service of the needs of the community face a fate similar to the one that befell this couple. This story calls to mind Judas' selling Jesus for thirty pieces of silver. In consequence, Judas falls off a precipice, his bowels break open, and he dies (Acts 1:15–20).

These themes come to expression in the rest of Acts. The church elects the deacons to see that all widows in the community receive a share of the community's material resources (Acts 6:1–6). The church is to embody justice in its material life.

When a famine creates hardship for believers in Judea, the disciples in Antioch "determined that according to their ability, each would send relief to the believers living in Judea" by means of Barnabas and Saul (Acts 11:27–30). This offering demonstrates that community relationships extend beyond the local congregations. The material support of congregations from different parts of the world for one another embodies the universal aspect of the restoration of the human community.

When he meets with the Ephesian elders, Paul emphasizes the communal ideal (Acts 20:17–35, especially 33–35). Paul has "coveted no one's silver or gold" but has worked with his own hands for his own support and to provide an example "that by such work we must support the weak." Paul quotes a saying of Jesus' that is not elsewhere recorded: "It is more blessed to give than to receive" (cf. Lk. 6:38).

Other stories in Acts call attention to ways in which preoccupation with wealth corrupts self and social world. Simon, a Samaritan magician who is converted, offers the disciples money so that he can have the power to dispense the Holy Spirit. The disciples admonish him to repent (Acts 8:14–24). When Paul and Silas exorcise a Philippian slave girl, her owners become incensed because they lost "their hope of making money" through the girl. They unjustly drag Paul and Silas before the authorities (Acts 16:16–24).

The connection between greed and injustice is again shown when Felix, with Paul in prison, hopes that Paul will offer the governor some money (Acts 24:24–26). This behavior is in marked contrast to Paul, who has a Jewish understanding of these matters (24:17).

Christian Relationships Today with Material Resources, Poverty, and Abundance

The Jewish tradition in which the author of Luke–Acts writes helps us to identify twin dangers associated with material resources: poverty and idolatry. On the one hand, the theme calls us to recognize that poverty detracts from the full-bodied life of blessing that God wishes for all in the human community. In the Lukan perspective, the church is to witness to God's will for all in the community to experience abundance of life by taking actions that express solidarity with people in poverty, by providing concrete help, and by aiming to change circumstances that create and sustain poverty. When the church shares its material resources with the poor, the church demonstrates God's desire for all to know abundance and to be freed from the enervation of living from day to day.

While the preceding observations may seem obvious, my impression is that many middle-class people in European American churches seldom encounter poverty in a personal way. Many middle-class European Americans live in areas of towns and cities far removed from massive, grinding deprivation. I know a few such people, living in gated housing developments in the suburbs, who avoid driving through ghetto areas on their way to work downtown. Some Christians even construct theological rationales to explain that God wills certain people to be poor. The preacher faces significant challenges in trying to help such people allow poverty into their consciousness and to own their role in covenantal community so that the community may provide abundantly for all.

On the other hand, many rich people continue to regard wealth idolatrously. While this tendency is easy to spot in the case of the super-wealthy of today's world, many people in the North American middle class manifest an idolatry involving fewer dollars and lower-priced merchandise, but that still makes possessions an organizing center of our world. Luke–Acts helps us name this tendency, to come face-to-face with its consequences, and to take the positive steps of repentance and communal sharing to relieve us of idolatry and bring us into participation in the realm of God.

At its heart, Jewish tradition presumes that a community witnessing to the realm of God does not simply give things (e.g., money, possessions, and various kinds of opportunities) to the poor, but enters into relationship with the poor. In regard to poverty, wealth, and abundance, Luke–Acts envisions the church as a community that does not give handouts but joins hands with the poor. The members of the early church in

Jerusalem partake of one another's lives day-to-day. Their sharing of physical resources provides material help (for both the poor and the rich) and symbolizes their deeper awareness of being joined as eschatological community. Many preachers will be stretched as we try to help congregations move from a handout mentality to perceiving the church as a community in which we are in genuine relationship with poor and rich.

The author of Luke–Acts presumes that the economic order of the Roman Empire will continue until the apocalypse. The prevailing economic system not only allowed for the continuation of poverty but also benefited from it because poverty provides cheap labor. The established system also sanctioned the idolatry of wealth and other abuses. Within this existing economic life, the Lukan church models an alternative covenantal understanding of the relationship among material resources, poverty, abundance, and community. To be sure, the church today must do at least as much.

Today's church needs further to call attention to the inequities in the distribution and symbolism of material resources that result from the contemporary North American version of capitalism. We cannot create the realm of God by better distributing material resources. But our economic life could be structured in ways that promote a greater community of abundance for all than at present. The church could help the larger social world to recognize difficulties inherent in our present system and to consider alternatives.

Luke–Acts envisions an optimum level of material sharing that goes far beyond that which is practiced by most contemporary North American congregations. Each household in our churches tends to provide for its own security and then to make a donation to the community as a means of contributing to the security of others. However, Acts 2:44–47 and 4:32–37 portray a community in which security is established for each household and for the community itself as people place their personal resources in a common treasury. As the preceding discussion of the theme in Luke's materials makes clear, God uses this communalism as a means of mediating providential care to all members of the community. The poor are relieved from the anxiety of living from day-to-day, while the rich are relieved from the anxiety of trying to amass wealth.

The incipient Jerusalem community is a vision toward which the church can move as it seeks to witness to the realm of God through the structures of its own material life. Few people in today's congregations are immediately ready to sell their property and to place it in a common treasury. However, the preacher is called to help people begin to explore such possibilities. My intuition is that many people are sufficiently ravaged by the roller coaster of economic life in North America that they are willing to imagine alternative ways of organizing our material world. Even when the economy is fairly robust, we are aware that the good times are not shared by all—the poor are still poor—and we realize an economic downturn will come. Such uncertainty may help create a climate of receptivity for imagining new patterns of economic life and the use of material resources.

A Sermon on the Theme of Poverty, Abundance, and Material Resources

The movie *Food for Thought* begins with a car pulling into a parking spot at a fast-food restaurant. The driver enters the restaurant and gets a sandwich, french fries, and a drink. The driver carries the tray to a booth, puts his sunglasses around the drink, and takes several minutes returning to the crowded counter to get ketchup, a straw, and napkins.

The driver returns to the booth. Surprise. Another person is in the booth eating the sandwich. The plastic top is off the drink. The french fries are spread across the tray.

The driver says nothing, but sits down, looks the other person defiantly in the eye, and eats a french fry. The other person, maintaining silence, looks back, eats a fry, then takes a bite of the sandwich. The driver picks up the sandwich, takes a bite, pulls out a straw, inserts it in the cup, and takes a long drink. This silent pattern continues until the last french fry is gone and the cup is empty.

The driver returns to the car and reaches for sunglasses. Not there. Returning to the restaurant, the driver goes to the booth. Oops. In the booth next to the one in which the two persons were sitting is a tray with a sandwich still in the wrapper, a box of almost fresh french fries, and a full drink with the driver's sunglasses around them.

Luke would understand this problem: people misperceiving material goods, taking things that aren't theirs, and not even being aware of it.

In Eden they had neither poverty nor wealth. But all had in abundance. No one ate off anyone else's tray. And the abundance was material. We learn this from Eden: God wants life to be a kind of garden in which we material beings are surrounded by material things that we use in order to serve God's purposes.

In Eden everybody had enough of everything, until the serpent prompted the first couple to eat the forbidden fruit. The first human beings misused the material fruit. Ever since, the human community has struggled with our relationship to material things.

Jewish people continued to remember life as it had been in Eden. Many of them, including the author of Luke, looked for the day when God would restore the world as a garden. In the meantime, Luke helps us get through.

On the one hand, we need material things. People suffer when they don't have enough material goods: Food. Clothing. Housing. Transportation. Medicine. God calls Israel to provide for widows, orphans, strangers, and many other poor people. The prophets considered the care of the poor so important that they used the condition of the poor as an index by which to gauge the spiritual health of the community. A community is unfaithful when people are hungry, poorly clothed, living in shacks, in ill health, and exploited. Such a community is rotting from the inside out and is on its way to collapse.

Luke calls the church to participate in this tradition by caring for the poor. "Whoever has two coats must share with anyone who has none" (Lk. 3:11). "Sell your possessions, and give alms" (12:33). "When you give…a dinner…invite the poor, the crippled, the lame, and the blind" (14:12–13). "Half of my possessions…I will give to the poor" (19:8). When Jerusalem was in famine, the disciples elsewhere "determined that…each would send relief to the believers living in Judea" (Acts 11:29). "By our work we must support the weak" (20:35, author's trans.).

These practices serve multiple purposes. They provide practical help for the poor. They help all members of the community to feel solidarity with one another—rich, poor, middle class. They help us anticipate the day when the world will again be a garden.

On the other hand, sometimes we want material things so much that we live for them. In Bible days some rich people wanted to acquire things so desperately that their acquisitiveness became an idol. They accumulated things for themselves while the poor went hungry. Sometimes the wealthy actively mistreated the poor. Sometimes they mistreated the poor by neglect. Either way, hungry is hungry. Such a community is rotting from the inside out and is on its way to collapse.

Luke resonates with the Jewish tradition by trying to help free wealthy people from the grip of greed by warning them about the dangers of wealth and by encouraging them to share their resources. "Woe to you who are rich, for you have received your consolation" (Lk. 6:24). "'You fool! This very night your soul is being demanded of you. And the things you have prepared, whose will they be?' So it is with those who store up treasures for themselves but are not rich toward God" (12:20–21). "It is easier for a camel to go through the eye of a needle than for someone who is rich to enter the [dominion] of God" (Lk. 18:25). "'Why has Satan filled your heart…to keep back part of the proceeds of the land?'…When Ananias heard these words, he fell down and died" (Acts 5:3, 5). Greed has a stiff price. We become the walking dead.

Luke's most striking contribution to this discussion is the memory of the early church. "No one claimed private ownership of any possessions, but everything they owned was held in common…There was not a needy person among them, for as many as owned lands or houses sold them and brought the proceeds of what was sold. They laid it at the apostles' feet, and it was distributed to each as any had need" (Acts 4:32–35).

Early Christian practice does not return the community to the garden of Eden, but it helps with both the poor and the rich. It provides for the poor. "There was not a needy person among them." This practice also frees the rich from idolizing money.

Few of us are ready to sell our goods and put them in a common treasury. But isn't it intriguing to think about this possibility? Wouldn't you like to be a part of a community in which no one is needy or greedy? Imagining such possibilities is a beginning. If we don't imagine that things can be different, probably they never will be.

I know some congregations who are taking steps in the direction of working with the poor, relieving the rich, and living more communally. Compared with the reports from Luke and Acts, these steps are small, but they are a start.

A few years ago, a layperson in Texas gave $2,000 to start a loan fund in the congregation. People can borrow interest-free to pay for emergencies. All they have to do is pay it back. Today, that fund has grown to more than $50,000.

A growing number of congregations sponsor soup kitchens and food pantries. If I woke up hungry and had no money and no job, I would like to know that a meal was coming. Most of these ministries operate on a donation basis. Church members give their time or their money or their cans of food. They come to the church and prepare the food and then stand behind a serving line, dish up the food, and go home. But Central Christian Church (Disciples of Christ) in downtown Indianapolis goes a step further in the direction of the Lukan church. The middle-class folk who prepare the meal sit at table with the hungry and homeless. All eat together. They talk with one another. A new world? No. But people are gradually feeling a greater sense of connection and commitment with and to one another.

I have heard of several households who buy houses on the same block. They share childcare, meal preparation, laundry, vegetable gardens, lawn care, automobiles, and dreams. It may not quite be owning all things in common, but they assume daily responsibility for one another.

One of my friends from seminary went in together with several other people in North Carolina to buy land jointly. They support themselves by working the land together and by working at jobs outside. They refurbished the old farmhouse, and they turned a barn into housing. Day by day they study the Bible and pray together, prepare meals, and engage in service projects in nearby towns. When my spouse and I were co-pastors and had a troubled youth in our congregation, we sent that youth to live in this community in North Carolina. The youth came back restored for relationship and life.

Such practices will not make this world into a garden of abundance for all. But they can help us imagine that our world can be different. They help move us toward a time when we will not eat off one another's trays. They help move us toward a world of abundance for all. What steps can you take in this direction?

Luke–Acts in the Revised Common Lectionary

The list below shows where passages from the Revised Common Lectionary are discussed.[1] I list all passages from Luke–Acts in the lectionary. The lectionary references are to the day(s) and year (A, B, or C) when the passages appear. For discussion of Luke–Acts and the lectionary, see pp. 32–34.

141

NOTES

Introduction

[1]Robert Karris, *What Are They Saying About Luke-Acts? A Theology of the Faithful God* (New York: Paulist Press, 1979).

[2]Ronald J. Allen, "Preaching on a Theme from the Bible," *Pulpit Digest* 75, no. 526 (1994): 78–86; *Handbook of Themes for Preaching*, ed. James W. Cox (Louisville, Ky.: Westminster/John Knox Press, 1991).

[3]For systematic discussion of many of these matters, see my chapters on Luke and Acts in *The Chalice Introduction to the New Testament*, ed. Dennis Smith (St. Louis: Chalice Press, forthcoming).

Chapter 1: Interpreting Luke–Acts

[1]Luke Timothy Johnson, *The Gospel of Luke,* Sacra Pagina 3 (Collegeville, Minn.: Liturgical Press, 1991), 9. For a countervailing view that regards Luke and Acts as different genres, see Richard Pervo, *Profit with Delight: The Literary Genre of the Acts of the Apostles* (Philadelphia: Fortress Press, 1987). Pervo regards Acts as a Hellenistic novel.

[2]For examples of Jewish apologetic literature in this mode, see Josephus, *The Jewish War* (which encourages the Jewish people to see *themselves* in the positive manner described in the text), as well as his *Against Apion* and *Antiquities of the Jews; The Letter of Aristeas;* and Philo (e.g., *Hypothetica, Against Flaccus, Embassy to Gaius*). Although not apologies, the Wisdom of Solomon and Ecclesiasticus (sometimes called Sirach or Ben Sira) seek to reinforce the Jewish self-consciousness of communities in the diaspora.

[3]Johnson, *Gospel of Luke*, 9.

Chapter 2: Preaching from Luke–Acts

[1]For this approach to preaching, see Ronald J. Allen, *Interpreting the Gospel: An Introduction to Preaching* (St. Louis: Chalice Press, 1998).

[2]Ibid., 82–95.

[3]I typically phrase this criterion, "Is the witness of the theme or text appropriate to the gospel?" In the context of discussion of theological method, I use the term *gospel* to refer to a concise summary of the heart of the good news from God for the world and the church. However, *gospel* can also refer to the literary genre of the books of Matthew, Mark, Luke, John, and several noncanonical writings. For the sake of clarity, in this book I avoid the former use of the term and speak synonymously of "the core of Christian conviction."

[4]David Kelsey, *Proving Doctrine: The Uses of Scripture in Modern Theology* (Harrisburg, Penn.: Trinity Press International, 1999), 170–74.

⁵For development of this approach, see Stephen Farris, *Preaching That Matters: The Bible and Our Lives* (Louisville, Ky.: Westminster John Knox Press, 1998).

⁶See the bibliography in the Introduction, note 2.

⁷For example, see Thomas Boomershine, *Story Journey: An Invitation to the Gospel as Storytelling* (Nashville: Abingdon Press, 1988).

Chapter 3: Preaching on the Realm of God

¹I do not mean to leave the impression that all Jewish apocalyptic theologians of the Hellenistic age subscribed to the following summary in every detail. These theologians, like theologians in every age, were not of a single mind. They articulate multiple viewpoints on numerous matters of interpretation. I intend only a broad sketch of the main lines of this movement.

²For example, Josephus, *Jewish Antiquities*, books 1–4, trans. H. St. J. Thackeray, Loeb Classical Library (Cambridge, Mass.: Harvard University Press, 1928), vol. 4, 2–3; cf. Lucian of Samosata, *How To Write History*, 23, trans. K. Kilburn. Loeb Classical Library (Cambridge, Mass.: Harvard University Press, 1968), vol. 6, 32–35.

³For bibliography, see chapter 5, note 1.

⁴This view of divine power is obviously indebted to relational (process) philosophy and theology. See, for example, Clark M. Williamson, *Way of Blessing, Way of Life: A Christian Theology* (St. Louis: Chalice Press, 1999), 103–11, passim.

Chapter 4: Preaching on the Holy Spirit

¹In order to understand the Spirit in Judaism, we should investigate the perception of the Spirit in each distinct theological trajectory of Judaism, with comparison and contrast. However, space does not permit such a consideration.

²Indeed, these functions do not belong exclusively to the Spirit. Some Jewish texts envision similar qualities in Wisdom, the Logos, Torah, the Shekinah, and the direct movement of God in the world.

³E. R. Dodds, *The Greeks and the Irrational* (Berkeley: University of California Press, 1951), 64–101. Dodds describes four common types of religious ecstasy (for which he uses the term *madness*) in the Hellenistic world: prophetic ecstasy, in which the prophet enters a trance and receives a vision; ritual ecstasy, in which the ritual intends to invoke the gods to grant fertility and other things; poetic ecstasy, in which the ecstatics are visited by the Muses; and erotic ecstasy, in which the human beings are united with the deity by means of sexual acts that take place in a sacred context.

⁴Blasphemy against the Holy Spirit will not be forgiven (Lk. 12:10). Blasphemy against the Spirit is denying that the ministry of Jesus and the church comes from God (Acts 7:51).

⁵Communal conversation, as in Acts 15, is only one means by which the Spirit operates. It also imparts visions, moves people to ecstasy, speaks through the voice of a single prophet, and so on. While there are multiple modes of the Spirit's operation, their authenticity is always gauged by the degree to which they lead the community into fuller awareness of the realm of God.

⁶This very thing is confirmed in Luke 20:22–34 and 21:11.

Chapter 5: Preaching on the Great Reunion of the Human Community

[1]Cf. Marc Shapiro, "Noachic Laws," *The Oxford Dictionary of the Jewish Religion*, ed. R. J. Zwi Weblowsky and Geoffrey Wigoder (New York: Oxford University Press, 1997), 504–5. For a rabbinic discussion of these laws, see Sanhedrin 56a–b, trans. Jacob Shachter, *The Babylonian Talmud*, ed. I. Epstein (London: Soncino Press, 1935), vol. 23, 381–82.

[2]*First Enoch* 10:18–22, in *The Old Testament Pseudepigrapha: Apocalyptic Literature and Testaments*, ed. James H. Charlesworth, trans. E. Isaac (New York: Doubleday, 1983), vol. 1, 18–19.

[3]For example, *1 Enoch* 50:2–5; 90:30; 91:41; *2 Baruch* 72:46; *Jubilees* 1:15; *Testament of Levi* 4:4; 18:9; *Testament of Judah* 22:9; 24:6; *Testament of Zebulon* 9:8; *Testament of Dan* 6:7; *Testament of Asher* 7:3.

[4]Josephus, *Antiquities of the Jews*, 18:29–30, trans. Louis H. Feldman, Loeb Classical Library (Cambridge, Mass.: Harvard University Press, 1931), vol. 9, 25–27.

[5]E. P. Sanders, *Jesus and Judaism* (Philadelphia: Fortress Press, 1985), 177.

Chapter 6: Preaching on the Restoration of Women

[1]Kiddushin 82b, trans. H. Freedman, in *The Babylonian Talmud*, ed. I. Epstein (London: Soncino Press, 1936), vol. 18, 425.

[2]Sotah 21b, trans. A. Cohen, in *The Babylonian Talmud*, ed. I. Epstein (London: Soncino Press, 1936), vol. 16, 109.

[3]Marcus Barth, *"Ephesians 4–6,"* The Anchor Bible (Garden City, N.Y.: Doubleday, 1974), 656.

[4]Jacob Neusner, *How the Rabbis Liberated Women,* University of South Florida Studies in the History of Judaism (Atlanta: Scholars Press, 1998), vii. For examples of literature reaching similar conclusions, cf. *Recovering the Role of Women: Power and Authority in Rabbinic Jewish Society*, ed. Peter Hass, University of South Florida Studies in the History of Judaism (Atlanta: Scholars Press, 1992); *"Women Like This": New Perspectives on Jewish Women in the Greco–Roman World*, Society of Biblical Literature: Early Judaism and Its Literature, ed. Amy–Jill Levine (Atlanta: Scholars Press, 1991).

[5]Bernadette J. Brooten, *Women Leaders in the Ancient Synagogue*, Brown Judaic Studies 36 (Chico, Calif.: Scholars Press, 1982).

[6]For an argument that the Lukan author intends to reinforce the view that the roles of women should be restricted, even subordinate, see Jane Schaberg, "Luke," in *The Women's Bible Commentary,* expanded ed., ed. Carol A. Newsom and Sharon H. Ringe (Louisville, Ky.: Westminster John Knox Press, 1998), 363–80; Gail R. O'Day, "Acts," in the aforementioned volume also maintains that Acts offers a limited view of the role of women in Christian community, 394–402. For other discussions of the ambiguities in Luke's perspectives, see Turid Karlsen Seim, "The Gospel of Luke," and Clarice J. Martin, "The Acts of the Apostles," in *Searching the Scriptures: A Feminist Commentary*, ed. Elisabeth Schüssler Fiorenza (New York: Crossroad, 1994), 728–62, 763–99, respectively.

[7]This latter interpretation is inspired by Addison G. Wright, "The Widow's Mites: Praise or Lament? A Matter of Context," *Catholic Biblical Quarterly* 44 (1982): 256–65.

[8]Robin Scroggs, "Paul and the Eschatological Woman," *Journal of the American Academy of Religion* 42 (1972): 283–303.

[9]The quoted phrase is from Sally Purvis, *The Stained Glass Ceiling: Churches and Their Women Pastors* (Louisville, Ky.: Westminster John Knox Press, 1995).

[10]Mary Donovan Turner and Mary Lin Hudson, *Saved from Silence: Finding Women's Voice in Preaching* (St. Louis: Chalice Press, 1999).

Chapter 7: Preaching on Poverty, Abundance, and the Use of Material Resources

[1]For example, Philo, "Every Good Man is Free," 84–87, *Philo*, trans. F. H. Coalson, Loeb Classical Library (Cambridge: Harvard University Press, 1935), vol. 9, 59–61; Josephus, *The Jewish War*, book 2: 122–23, Loeb Classical Library, trans. H. St. J. Thackeray (Cambridge, Mass.: Harvard University Press, 1926), vol. 2, 369–70.

[2]Friedrich Hauck, "*koinonos,*" in *Theological Dictionary of the New Testament*, vol. 3, ed. Gerhard Kittel and Gerhard Friedrich, trans. Geoffrey W. Bromiley (Grand Rapids, Mich.: Eerdmans, 1965), 789–809.

[3]Luke Timothy Johnson, *Sharing Possessions: Mandate and Symbol of Faith*, Overtures to Biblical Theology (Philadelphia: Fortress Press, 1981).

Appendix: Luke–Acts in the Revised Common Lectionary

[1]The table lists only the readings that are designated for preaching. It does not list passages in Luke–Acts that are designated as passages or alternate passages for liturgical use–Luke 1:47–55 (Advent 3 AB, Advent 4 BC); Luke 1:68–79 (Advent 2 C, Reign of Christ).